IN FULL BLOOM

IN FULL BLOOM

Tales of Women in Their Prime

Sharon Creeden

August House Publishers, Inc.
LITTLE ROCK

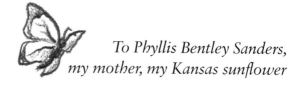

*To Phyllis Bentley Sanders,
my mother, my Kansas sunflower*

Published 1999 by August House, Inc.,
P.O. Box 3223, Little Rock, Arkansas, 72203.
501-372-5450.

Printed in the United States of America.

10 9 8 7 6 5 4 3 2 1 HB

LIBRARY OF CONGRESS CATALOGING-IN-PUBLICATION DATA
Creeden, Sharon, 1938–
In full bloom: tales of women in their prime / Sharon Creeden.
        p.   cm.
Includes bibliographical references.
ISBN 0-87483-576-3 (pbk. : alk. paper)
1. Women—Folklore. 2. Women—Biography. I. Title.
GR470.C74 1999
398.2'082—dc21   99-32891
                              CIP

Executive editor: Liz Parkhurst
Project editor: Joy Freeman
Cover and interior art: Cici Davidson
Cover and book design: Joy Freeman

AUGUST HOUSE PUBLISHERS

CONTENTS

NOT ROSES

FOREWORD

by Naomi Baltuck

Half a lifetime ago, I heartily embraced storytelling as an art, a profession, and a way of life, and knew that I had finally found my path. I was delighted to be able to mine the incredible wealth of wisdom, the precious legacy of stories that had been passed down from countless generations. There were so many tales to tell: tales to teach, to heal, to entertain. Stories helped me make sense of the world, and through the stories, I had a valuable gift to pass on to others. But along the way, it dawned on me that the lion's share of folktales spotlight the *hero's* journey. A good heroine, in fact, was hard to find (you always get the other kind). There were plenty of Sleeping Beauties—nice girls, to be sure—but the majority of women with any true brains or backbone were cruel stepmothers, wicked witches, and old hags.

Most of today's world cultures are patriarchal, and too many women have learned to go directly to the back of the bus. "A virtuous girl," they say in India, "is the girl who suffers and dies without a sound." In Spain they say, "A good wife, an injured leg, and a pair of torn trousers should stay at home." In Argentina, "A woman who knows Latin will neither find a husband nor come to a good end." Men are taught to apologize for their weaknesses, women for their strengths. Even so, I began searching for stories of unapologetic women, strong, clever, and courageous, who take an active and decisive role in their own fate. Those were the stories I favored, but when I became the mother of two daughters, my preference for positive female role models became a passion, a *necessity*.

Ironically, it was the women—most often the grandmothers—who would pass on the old tales to their daughters and grand-daughters, while stirring the porridge, softening a deerskin hide, or working a spindle by the light of the fire. In the late eighteenth and nineteenth centuries, circumstances converged that threatened to displace women as the repositories of culture and wisdom. The process of printing became more affordable and literacy more common among the middle class, and at the same time a wave of nationalism swept over the world. Folklorists went out in droves to collect and publish their homelands' oral traditions. But, of course, the collectors were all males from male-dominated cultures, and most of their informants were women. Those simple illiterate women must have been reluctant to share stories that they feared would not meet with the approval of the educated strangers who came to record them.

In Africa, there are instances where female informants confessed to having withheld their stories for fear of being ridiculed. At any rate, it is unlikely that the collectors placed any particular value upon the exploits of women and girls. We can only wonder how many of those stories were judged by those men to be trivial and irrelevant and, as such, were passed over. Other collectors, such as the brothers Grimm, are known to have tampered with traditional tales to reinforce their own values. The good news is that, although there is still a relative dearth of feminist folktales, this need is now more widely recognized and is being addressed with a growing number of collections that celebrate spirited women.

Our society has made a few small leaps for womankind since women won the vote. Credit where credit is due: we are *trying* to do the right thing. The Susan B. Anthony dollar just never quite found its way into circulation, but we are trying again with a Sacagawea coin. Barbie Dolls now come in all colors, and there is even a Wheelchair Barbie (although her wheelchair doesn't fit through the door of her pink plastic house). Today we can buy out-fits and dress her up as a doctor, an airline pilot, or an Olympic ath-lete. But beneath it all, she is still Barbie (44-18-26), and far too top-heavy in those spiked heels to ever really be able to "run with the wolves."

The fact is that America worships youth and beauty, kowtows to anorexic models and Hollywood bombshells. At twenty, Brooke

Shields mourned for her lost youth. In Hollywood, writers over thirty are considered over the hill and many are forced to adopt false identities in order to sell a script. And as a generation of baby-boomers begins to show the wear and tear of middle age, many follow Cher's example, and are saving their pennies for tummy tucks, nose jobs, liposuction, and facelifts. Too many of today's women have accepted society's judgement and allow their aging bodies, not their timeless spirits, to become the definition of who they are.

With every bend in the road, needs and standards change for a society as well as for the individual, and so must the stories that we look to for guidance and inspiration. America—and I do not mean only the men—needs to take another big step towards enlightenment. And perhaps that should be a step backward. Back to a time when our elderly were not packed off to nursing homes to die, but instead were given an honored place at the hearth. Back to a time when stretchmarks, crow's feet, and age spots were badges of endurance, and commanded the respect due a sage survivor. Back to a time when old age was an outward sign of an inner wisdom acquired through many lifetimes of experience, an accumulation of lore passed down from generation to generation.

There is a proverb from Rwanda that says, "No woman without a big sister." But in today's mobile society, the extended family is the exception, and our access to the elderly wisewoman is often limited. Vi Hilbert, an Upper Skagit elder and storyteller, says, "Our stories tell us who we are." We never outgrow our need for stories. More than ever we need our elders to teach by example, and we need their stories to use as guiding stars along the spiritual journey of our lives. We must reclaim those "elder tales" that affirm our value, demonstrate the art of aging gracefully, and direct us toward a healthy, hopeful old age. Otherwise we will become a generation of defeated, bitter old women who believe that each new wrinkle detracts from our worth as human beings.

If stories about feisty young heroines are hard to find, stories that celebrate women in their maturity are even more elusive. So when Sharon Creeden first told me that she was writing a book called *In Full Bloom: Tales of Women in Their Prime*, I told her, "Yes, yes! The world needs a book like that." When Sharon put the manuscript into my hands, I read it in one sitting, and thought, "Yes, yes, *I* need a book like this."

For as long as I have known her—and that is nearly two decades—Sharon has always struck me as being a lively mix of sugar and spice—a little sugar, a lot of spice. Her spiritual life is rich and deep, yet she balances this with a healthy amount of grit and earthiness.

The path Sharon has followed through life has at times been well worn, and at other times, less traveled. As an Air Force wife and stay-at-home mom, she attended P.T.A. meetings, was den mother to her son's scout troop, had her own troop of Campfire Girls, and sent homemade cookies to the school bake sales. Yet after her children were grown, she also attended law school, became a prosecuting attorney, and achieved success in what has traditionally been considered a "man's world." But Sharon discovered what so many women never do—that successfully competing against men in their world does not necessarily move a woman forward on the path to self-fulfillment as a woman. Eventually she found her place as an award-winning author and storyteller, where she can integrate both her active, logical, masculine side, and her intuitive, emotional, feminine side.

Sharon is a wild rose in full bloom, with one toe deeply rooted in the earth, and an ear bent toward Heaven. This balance of the traditional and the non-conventional, spirituality and earthiness, reverence and irreverence, has found its way into this book. Sharon has chosen her stories well, and she has included tales that focus on all aspects and stages of the mature Heroine's Journey. She employs a unique combination of myth and folktale, legend and history. This pairing of ancient folk wisdom with examples of true flesh and blood history makes these stories more relevant to real women.

Sharon has drawn from the treasure trove of world folktales that highlights those facets of womanhood that are universal, facets that can shine as beacons for each of us as we make our way along the Heroine's Journey. But just as crucially, Sharon challenges us to dig down into the good American soil to rediscover our roots. Barbie is a freak, an accident, a digression; we must pull her down from her pink plastic pedestal and reclaim our identity as *American women*. And what is it that makes us uniquely American? Surely it is our connection to the land, our pioneering spirit of adventure, our stubborn refusal to be dominated, the unending fight for freedom and justice against all odds and at any cost. *These* are the qualities of the women we must venerate and emulate. Their stories can provide a source of courage, strength, and inspiration to carry us past life's milestones, as well as through the daily struggles. When we come to a rough spot in the road, we need only steel ourselves and recall how Grandmother rescued the seed corn. When our loved ones need protection, we can throw back our shoulders and, like Oonagh MacCool and Edith Bolling Wilson, take on the offending giant. When we come to a fork in the road, perhaps we will take heart from the stories of Biddy Early and Poker Alice, and be inspired to flout convention and take the less traveled road.

That is the American Way. And what is the Real American Woman made of? Take a little sugar, a lot of spice, salt of the earth, a splash of vinegar, and a liberal dose of fine spirits that can only improve with age.

As the old woman said when asked about the burden of growing old, "Consider the alternative…" Besides, as you will find when you read this book, there is a certain freedom that comes with age. In Africa, the Mamprusi say, "If you see an old woman chasing a rabbit, you can be fairly certain that she has already caught more than one." I want to be like that old woman. When my time comes—and I know it is just around the next bend or two—I want to approach my latter years with passion and hope. I want to use my precious time on earth to make my peace with myself and others. I want to do well by doing good. I want to face with courage those battles that must be fought and, when necessary, to accept defeat with good grace. Most importantly, I want never, never to be afraid to look ahead.

The gift of this book is to help women everywhere to remember, through the stories of those who have come before, who we are and where we are going, and to remind us of all the glorious possibilities that we hold in the palm of our hand. I will put it on my medicine shelf and refer to it often.

INTRODUCTION

More than a decade ago, I began my quest for stories of mature women. One reason was professional: as a storyteller, I was telling less to children's groups and more to women's groups. Women wanted to hear stories about women. The second reason was personal: I sought guidance from stories about women who had lived through the experiences which I was living.

First, I chose folktales, because they are my storyteller's staple. Folktales give access to centuries of accumulated wisdom, provide diverse examples of female heroism, and portray archetypal women—such as the goddess Demeter, eternal essence of motherhood. Speaking on a symbolic level, folktales plunge us into the depths of life's universal themes—including childbirth, aging, and death.

I searched through hundreds of folktales to finally settle on thirty. After consulting variants from cultures around the world, I refashioned these tales with my own words and embellishments. In the tradition of storytelling, I never leave a story the way I find it.

Next, I paired each folktale with a vignette about a notable American woman. Looking at both mythical and real women provides a rich context for viewing women's lives. Biographies inform us on a practical level by showing real women triumphing over the challenges of adulthood. For example, on the theme of wife abuse, the Hawaiian myth about Hina is paired with a biographical sketch about Tina Turner. The myth of Hina climbing to the moon to escape her husband may touch our souls. But we relate personally to Tina Turner's escape from abuse: we have seen the movie *What's Love Got to Do with It*, we have sung her songs, we have imagined our legs look as good as hers.

Frequently the distinction between biographies and folktales blurs; it is sometimes difficult to distinguish where history ends and myth begins. Incidents from the lives of real women such as Elizabeth of Hungary become mythical. Centuries of retelling and embellishment by the Catholic Church altered the stories of saints such as Brigid of Ireland. Even modern women such as Marie Laveau and Mae West seem more legendary than real—Laveau through superstition and hearsay and West through her own publicity.

Whether in folklore or history, the women in this book are larger than life, personifying cunning, courage, and compassion. They are archetypal women—goddesses, queens, saints; they are everyday women—mothers, widows, pioneers. They are our allies, examples, and mentors calling out to us, "I did it and so can you." As psychologist Kathleen Noble says, "We must tell the stories of courageous women so we will know that many women in many places throughout the course of time have dreamed 'impossible dreams' and made them a reality, and so inspire ourselves to do the same."[1]

How amazing to recognize our lives in the lives of heroic women. Their struggles resonate with us because they are also our struggles. Through storytelling, we can connect to the community of women who have lived since the first woman, Lilith.

The title *In Full Bloom* was inspired by daily walks along the waterfront park in front of my Seattle condominium. Tall rosebushes—*rosa rugosa*—flanked the path, flourishing in spite of raw weather and neglect. My habit was to pull magenta-colored petals from the flowers and carry them in my hands and pockets. I chose the open, collapsing roses, leaving the heads to become rose hips and the tight buds to blossom.

One day I read a quote by Jane Michelson: "Is the fully opened rose not as beautiful as the bud?"[2] By observing the seaside blossoms, I knew the answer to Michelson's question. I saw the beauty in the developed flower, which bestowed its frilly petals and intoxicating fragrance so generously.

To me, younger women are like firm, closed buds, prized by florists for their potential longevity, and containing the promise of fullness. Mature women are like fully open flowers—soft, voluminous, responsive to the wind, yielding to the touch. *In Full Bloom* is a celebration of mature women, as beautiful as the buds of their youth.

Roses

After long dreaming in the folded bud,
After long nights of waiting—ah, who knows
How joyous a surprise, to open wide
And find one's self—a rose!
—May Lewis[1]

Sybil Collins, my storytelling friend who is in her eighth decade, and I were having tea and scones at the Parknasilla Hotel, a seaside resort in Ireland. Standing indoors because of the rain, we looked out the tall windows on the sumptuous gardens.

Assuming that all women of age, in their infinite wisdom, instinctively knew the names of flowers, I pointed to a blooming tree. "What kind of flowers are those?" I asked.

Sybil, who often sounds like Mae West, wisecracked, "I know only two kinds of flowers—roses and not roses."

Yes! I thought. If there are two kinds of flowers, maybe there are two kinds of women—roses and not roses; traditional women and untraditional women. Roses are the beloved, idealized flowers; rose women are the beloved, idealized mothers, matriarchs, and saints.

The folktales and biographies in this first section tell of women who share the attributes of roses. Pleasing and nurturing, these women find personal fulfillment in traditional roles and relationships. They give time, counsel, and care to those around them. Some of these women are literally associated with roses. Elizabeth of Hungary's bread turned to roses, Mary Bethune was known as "the Black Rose," and Ted Kennedy called his mother "the most beautiful rose of all."

Even after its petals have fallen, a rose remains useful. The rose head forms a rose hip, a seeded fruit, which has served as a food source since prehistoric times. And so it is that even after conventional beauty and fertility fade, these women remain useful; they

19

hold the seeds for future generations. In the Rumanian folktale "The Wise Old Woman" (p. 91), the old woman who was considered useless and ordered abandoned, holds the wisdom to help her people survive famine. As Maggie Kuhn, founder of the Gray Panthers, said, "We are the elders of the tribe. We are concerned with the survival of the tribe, not of ourselves."[2]

SHARING OUR WEALTH

...Bread feeds the body indeed, but the flowers feed also the soul.

—The Koran

Bread and Roses

Hungary

During the thirteenth century, there lived a Hungarian princess who married a German duke, Ludwig of Thuringia. She was both beautiful and good, and her name was Elizabeth.

One year, famine came to the land; crops failed and cattle died. Elizabeth grieved to see people hungry when her castle larder was full of bounty. She ordered her husband's treasury and granaries opened. When she shared with the poor, Ludwig scolded her, "If you feed these lazy beggars, they will never work. God helps those who help themselves."

One day Elizabeth left the castle to visit the sick, hiding a basket of bread beneath her mantle. Her husband, returning from a hunt, saw his wife clutching her mantle around her. *She's smuggling my food to those lazy beggars,* he thought to himself. On the pretense of giving her a greeting kiss, he went to her. Throwing her mantle aside to see what she was hiding, the duke beheld a basket filled with roses. Who was more surprised—Ludwig or Elizabeth?

It was not the season of roses, and the duke marveled at the beauty of the flowers. He plucked a full-blown blossom to tuck in his hat and led his horse to the stable.

Wrapping her mantle around the basket, Elizabeth continued to the houses of the poor. Miracle of miracles—when she arrived, the basket was once again filled with the loaves of bread.

In the stable, the groomsmen smirked at the duke's headgear. "What are you laughing at?" asked the duke. Taking off his hat, he saw not the rose he had put there but a round loaf of freshly baked bread.

Ludwig, the Duke of Thuringia, was a smart man. He soon realized that the bread turning to roses was a miraculous sign of his wife's generous spirit. Instead of being embarrassed for wearing a loaf of bread on his hat, the duke repented his stingy ways. He erected a pillar at the site of the miracle and joined Elizabeth in caring for the sick and hungry.

Margaret Olivia Slocum Sage

1828–1918

Some women must wait until their miserly husbands die to practice charity. Margaret Olivia Slocum Sage became one of the United States' leading philanthropists, but only after her husband's death.

A traditional daughter and wife, Olivia Slocum was born in Syracuse, New York, in 1828 to a well-to-do family. At eighteen, she attended the Troy Female Seminary run by Emma Willard; after graduation, she taught school. At forty-five, she became the second wife of Russell Sage, a fifty-three-year-old self-made millionaire.

But Olivia Slocum had married a miser. The newlyweds didn't go on a honeymoon. The bride went to Russell Sage's house, where they retired to separate bedrooms. By marrying again, it turned out, he had saved the salary of a housekeeper.

The press reviled Sage for his parsimonious habits. He dressed in twelve-dollar suits, rode a trolley to his office, and carried his lunch. When Sage saw a newspaper photo of his petite, gray-haired wife feeding peanuts to squirrels in the park, he admonished her, "You could have used bread crumbs from the kitchen."[1]

Russell Sage did not believe in charity. When Olivia, a devoted churchgoer, pressured him to donate funds for a new church, Sage replied, "I will be happy to lend them the money—if they have acceptable co-signers."[2]

In 1906, his doctors persuaded the ailing millionaire to take his first vacation. Sage died on his vacation, perhaps as a result of too much leisure and too little work. Olivia Slocum was his sole heir. Her inheritance was never precisely revealed, but the estimated figure was $63 million. The headlines declared her "the richest woman in the world."[3]

First, Olivia splurged on a full-length Russian sable coat with matching hat and muff. She then spent the next twelve years giving away Sage's money. She bought seventy thousand acres on Marsh Island in the Gulf of Mexico and donated it to Louisiana as a bird sanctuary.[4] Her $1 million gift to her alma mater, Emma Willard's school, resulted in the founding of Russell Sage College in Troy, New York.

Her foundation, established in 1907, received the bulk of her money. She named the foundation after her husband, because she thought it was inappropriate for a woman to have her name on a public organization. When she announced the Russell Sage Foundation, Slocum said, "I am almost eighty years old and I am just beginning to live."[5] By the time of her death in 1918, she had given away $80 million.

SHIELDING
OUR HUSBANDS

*Every man who is high up loves to think he
has done it all himself; and the wife smiles, and
lets it go at that. It's our only joke, every
woman knows that.*

      —J.M. Barrie, *What Every Woman Knows*

The Cunning of Finn's Wife

Ireland

What Irish man, woman, or child has not heard of the great and
glorious giant, Finn MacCool. Finn and his wife Oonagh lived at
the top of Knockmany Hill. His neighbors wondered why Finn had
picked such a spot. "What were you thinking, Mr. MacCool, by
placing your home upon the top of Knockmany, where you are
never without a wind and where there is no water?"

"I placed it there because I'm fond of a good view, and what better view than from the peak of Knockmany?" replied MacCool.
But the real state of the case was, Finn wanted to keep a sharp
lookout for the giant Cucullin.

The giant Cucullin—some say he was Irish, and some say he was
a Scot—could stamp his foot and shake the country around him.
He carried all his strength in the middle finger of his right hand. He
carried in his pocket a thunderbolt that he had flattened to show
his power.

Cucullin had given every other giant in Ireland a beating—
except Finn MacCool. He swore he would never rest—night or day,
winter or summer—until he caught Finn. Finn, however, kept
dodging from place to place whenever he heard that Cucullin was
on his scent.

So it was that when Finn was out working on the Giant's
Causeway, he heard Cucullin was coming to have a trial of strength.

Finn was suddenly seized with warm affection for his wife and the need to tend to her "delicate health." He pulled up a fir tree, lopped off the roots and branches to make a walking stick, and set off home.

When Finn climbed to the top of Knockmany, he stuck his head in the door. "God save all here!" he called out.

"My dear Finn, you're welcome home to your own Oonagh." She gave him a playful slap that curled the lake water at the bottom of the hill. "What brings you home so soon?"

"Not a thing but the purest love and affection for yourself," replied Finn. But Oonagh knew there was something on his mind. It took two or three days of wheedling, but she finally learned his secret.

"It's this Cucullin that's troubling me," Finn finally admitted, and popped his thumb in his mouth. He had the thumb of prophecy and could foretell events by sucking on it. "He's coming!" cried Finn. "How will I manage? If I run, I'll be disgraced! If I stay I'll be flattened just like a thunderbolt!"

"When will he come?" said she.

He sucked harder. "My thumb tells me tomorrow at two o'clock."

Oonagh gave him a pat. "Well, my bully, don't be downcast. Depend on me and I'll bring you out of this scrape." Her promise relieved Finn, because if truth be told, his wife had got him out of many a quandary.

Oonagh took nine threads of different colors. Following a fairy spell, she plaited them into three braids with three colors each. She tied one round her right arm, one round her heart, and the third round her right ankle. "Now nothing I undertake can fail," she said to herself.

She sent round to the neighbors and borrowed one-and-twenty iron griddles. She kneaded one-and-twenty cakes of bread, tucked the iron griddles into the hearts of the cakes, and baked them in the usual way. She set these beside the regular cakes from the previous day. She made curds and whey out of a new pot of milk and shaped loaves of soft white cheese. She went onto the mountain and collected white stones. She brought out a cradle. It had belonged to their son, now grown and gone to live with the fairies. Then Oonagh sat down, quite content to wait for the arrival of the giant Cucullin.

The next day she spied Cucullin coming across the valley. She made up the cradle, dressed Finn like a baby, and tucked him under the covers. She put the white stones and freshly made cheese at his feet. "Just lie there snug and be guided by me," Oonagh warned.

Cucullin knocked loudly. "God save all here! Is Finn MacCool in the house?"

Oonagh opened the door. "Why, no, it's just me and the baby. Finn left in a fury after a giant named Cucullin. I pity that poor lump if Finn catches him."

"Well"—the giant pushed inside—"I'm Cucullin, and I won't rest 'til I get my hands on him."

"Oh, you poor creature, it will be a bad day for you if you do," said Finn's wife. "You're welcome to stay awhile. But first, would you be so civil as to turn the house around? When the wind blows in the door, Finn always turns the house around."

Cucullin went outside and took the measure of the task. He pulled his middle finger on his right hand until it cracked three times. Then he wrapped his arms about the house, lifted it up, and set it down where Oonagh told him. Finn, who was inside in the cradle, broke into a sweat and sucked his thumb.

Oonagh appeared nonchalant. "As you are so civil, maybe you'd oblige me further. Finn was about to drill for a spring when he took off after you. If you find it, I'll consider it a kindness."

She took Cucullin down to a solid rock. He cracked his right middle finger nine times. Stooping down, he drove his finger into the rock and tore a cleft four hundred feet down and a quarter-mile long. The spring that bubbled up is still known today as Lumford's Glen.

Though Cucullin's feat of strength threw Oonagh off her guard, she composed herself. "Come in and eat a bit." She set out a plate of the cakes that had the griddle irons concealed inside. Cucullin took a whack at one, let out a yowl, and spit out two teeth. "Blood and fury! What kind of bread is this?"

"That's Finn's bread," Oonagh answered. "Only he and the babe there in the cradle can eat it. I thought you might be able to manage it."

Not to be outdone, Cucullin bit into another cake. He yelped and spit out two more teeth.

Just then, Finn set up a howl. "I'm hungry, Ma!" Oonagh

handed him a cake with no griddle inside. Finn chomped it down. "More!"

Cucullin was thunderstruck. *If this is the son,* he thought, *I'm loathe to meet his dad.* He said, "What a big, strong boy."

"That he is! He can squeeze water from a stone," beamed Oonagh.

Baby Finn picked up a white stone from his cradle and threw it at Cucullin with a chuckle. Cucullin caught it. Finn picked up a cheese, which looked like a stone, and began squeezing it. Whey, as clear as water, oozed out. Not to be outdone by the baby, Cucullin squeezed his stone. Nothing happened.

Finn popped the cheese in his mouth, chewed, and swallowed it down. Cucullin followed suit, chewed, screamed, and spit out the remainder of his teeth. He started toward the cradle. "Let me see what kind of baby teeth can chew stone."

The giant stuck his finger in Finn's mouth—the middle finger of his right hand. Finn waited until the finger was full inside then bit down hard. He bit off Cucullin's magic finger. Finn hopped out of the cradle and began thumping on the poor, weak giant. Cucullin barely made off with his life.

Oonagh stood at the door, watching his departing hustle. She dusted her hands. "'Tis true, women's wit wins over muscle."

Edith Bolling Wilson

1872–1961

In the 1990s, some bumper stickers read IMPEACH HILLARY. In 1919, some bumper stickers—had they existed in those days—might have read IMPEACH EDITH. Edith Bolling Wilson, after all, actually did run the country. Sometimes it is not just an Irish giant who needs the artful aid of a spouse; sometimes it is the President of the United States.

Edith Bolling was the second wife of Woodrow Wilson, the twenty-eighth president. He was a widower and she a widow when they were introduced to each other by the president's cousin. Their courtship began during the president's first term and a year after the death of his first wife. Soon the president was writing Edith daily love letters. He proposed to her in May 1915, following a private dinner at the White House.

In December 1915, they married at her house in the presence of fifty friends. The new bride reported, "I wore plain black velvet with a velvet hat trimmed with goura, and had lovely orchids."[1]

Because women did not have the vote, Edith Wilson could not cast a ballot for her husband when he was reelected. However, she was at his side during the campaign. The president discussed affairs of state with her; they read diplomatic dispatches together.

In 1919, she traveled with him on a twenty-two-day train trip, while he delivered speeches in favor of the League of Nations. On September 26, the president developed a severe headache, which turned out to be the result of a minor stroke. The train sped back to Washington to the "blessed shelter of the White House," as Edith Wilson called it.[2]

For several days, the president paced in pain, unable to work. Then he collapsed with a massive stroke. His left side was paralyzed, his speech slurred, and his eyesight blurred. His body was incapacitated, but his mind was clear.

The president had eighteen months left in office. Should he resign? Secretary of State Robert Lansing said yes, but Vice President Thomas Marshall did not want the responsibility of being president. Edith Wilson, who knew of the unfinished fight for the League of Nations, thought the resignation would kill her husband.

The doctors predicted recovery if "the President were released from every disturbing problem during these days of Nature's effort to repair the damage done."[3] Edith Wilson organized the White House into a hospital. She sealed the Pennsylvania Avenue gate and posted Marine guards to screen visitors. Following the physicians' advice, she controlled access to the president and intercepted all correspondence.

During the day, she met with government officials, screened mail, memos, and documents, and identified the most urgent matters. In her autobiography, she described this period of convalescence:

> So began my stewardship. I studied every paper, sent from the different Secretaries or Senators, and tried to digest and present in tabloid form the things that, despite my vigilance, had to go to the President.[4]

In the evening, she sat by his bed and chatted with Wilson. When he was alert, she discussed business with him. If Wilson told her what to do, she wrote down his instructions. The documents from this period bear her handwritten comments: *The President instructs…*[5]

> I, myself, never made a single decision regarding the disposition of public affairs. The only decision that was mine was what was important and what was not, and the *very* important decision of when to present matters to my husband.[6]

Rumors circulated that the president was dead or insane and chained in the basement. Through October, November, and December, Edith Wilson maintained the cheerful ruse that the president was merely resting for a few days.

Some officials were convinced that Edith Wilson was running the nation. The president's chief assistant, Joseph Tumulty, said she was power-hungry. Senator Henry Cabot Lodge called her "the Iron Queen." One Republican senator labeled her "the Presidentress who had fulfilled the dream of the suffragettes by changing her title from First Lady to Acting First Man."[7]

By mid-December, Woodrow Wilson had recovered enough to receive official visitors and work a few hours each day. As the president resumed his duties, Edith Wilson withdrew from her "stewardship." He did not completely recover and was not nominated by his party in 1920. Warren Harding was elected president.

The Wilsons left the White House for a private home in Washington. Woodrow Wilson died in 1924. Edith Wilson, who had been called the "first woman president," lived a quiet, private life until her death at eighty-nine.

PROTECTING
OUR DAUGHTERS

Oh, what a power is motherhood, possessing
A potent spell. All women alike
Fight fiercely for a child.
—Euripides, *Iphigenia in Aulis*

Demeter and Persephone

Greece

In the ancient days of Greece, it was always summer. As the goddess of green and growing things, Demeter made the fields golden with wheat and the trees heavy with fruit. She was the mother of the earth and of her daughter, Persephone.

One bright day, far from her mother, Persephone frolicked in a grassy meadow. She gathered flowers—crocuses, roses, violets, irises, and lovely hyacinths.

One narcissus grew amid the profuse flowers. From its root grew a hundred radiant white blooms and it smelled most sweetly. "It is perfect!" cried Persephone. She reached out with both hands to pluck the astonishing flower. But the narcissus was a snare for the beautiful maiden; when she picked it, the earth split open before her.

Out of the gape rode Hades, the Lord of the Dead. He seized Persephone; though she struggled, he caught her up in his golden chariot. She screamed for her father, Zeus. She cried out for her mother.

While Persephone could still glimpse the bright sky, she was taken by force into the dark underworld. The earth closed above her and blocked out Helios, the sun, who sat aloof in his distant temple. Her pleas echoed off the mountain peaks and in the ocean's depths. And her queenly mother heard them.

31

A pang went through Demeter's heart. She set off in a panic, like a wild bird, over land and sea, to the place where she had last seen her beloved child. Gone! The rip in the earth had healed, and the bees and butterflies circled the flowers in the empty meadow.

"Persephone!" Demeter called out. When no answer came, Demeter ran screaming over the hills; birds and animals scattered before her. For nine days and nights, she circled the earth, searching. At night, she brandished shining torches to light the shadows.

Persephone was locked away from the shine of the torches and the sound of her mother's call. Hades crowned her queen and placed her upon a throne. She sat, clad in black with her golden hair fading, hoping for her mother's rescue.

But on the dawn of the tenth day, Hecate, goddess of the underworld and the dark of the moon, came to Demeter. "Who has taken my daughter?" Demeter asked.

Hecate replied, "I heard her cries, but I saw not who took her."

Demeter and Hecate went to the sun. "Helios! Pity me!" said Demeter. "I heard my daughter's voice, but I saw nothing. You see everything. Tell me, was it a god or a mortal who stole my daughter?"

"Queen Demeter, I will tell you the truth, for I pity your grief for your trim-ankled daughter. It was no mortal," Helios replied. "No one is guilty but Zeus. He gave her to Hades to be his bride."

Savage anguish rent the goddess's heart. "Zeus betrayed me?"

"Is it betrayal to give your daughter to such a desirable son-in-law? As king of the dead, Hades wields great power," said Helios. "I advise you to stop your weeping."

"I will not stop weeping and I will not dwell on Olympus with the immortals," said Demeter.

Disguised as a poor old woman, Demeter sought the company of mortals. She wandered to Eleusis and sank down by the roadside at the Well of the Maiden. King Celius's four daughters saw her when they came to draw water with their golden pitchers. "Where do you come from, old mother?" they asked.

"Fair maidens!" Demeter said. "Pirates seized me and brought me across the sea—but I escaped and, in my wandering, came here. Pity me, dear children. Please tell me where I can find work suited to an old woman. I could hold a newborn child in my arms and be a nurse."

"Wait, gentle woman, while we go to our mother, for she has a newborn child."

Swiftly the four ran to Queen Metaneira to tell her about the old woman by the well. The queen bade them bring the old woman to the palace. The princesses came bounding back with their skirts held high and their yellow hair streaming over their shoulders. Demeter followed them, her head covered with a veil and her heart aching for her own fair-haired daughter.

When Demeter stepped across the portal, her splendor shone in to the palace. The queen was filled with awe. "Here is my only son, Damophon," she said as she handed her son to the goddess.

Demeter raised the boy like a god. She fed him ambrosia instead of food and milk. She breathed sweetly as she held him on her lap. At night, in secret, she put him into the fire to make him immortal.

One night, the queen spied the rites and shrieked for Demeter to stop. The goddess turned, terrible in her brightness. She pulled the child from the fire and thrust him from her hands. "Senseless mortal! You don't know when fate is bringing you something good or something bad."

Then the goddess flung off her disguise. The light in her eyes filled the halls like a flash of lightning. "I am Demeter! I would have made your boy deathless," she raged. "Now to win back my favor, you must build me a temple." She left the palace.

Quickly, the Eleusinians built her temple. Demeter took her place inside, wasting away with longing for her daughter. The earth responded to her grief; the soil did not yield a single seed. "Nothing will grow until Persephone returns," Demeter vowed.

The earth did not take seed. Mortals began to starve. As Zeus watched from Mount Olympus, he began to fear that the earth and the people would die. There would be no more gifts and sacrifices. He sent golden-winged Iris, the goddess of the rainbow, to summon Demeter. Iris found her in her temple.

"Demeter!" she said. "Zeus calls you back to the family of gods." Demeter's heart was unmoved.

Zeus sent all the gods, but Demeter scorned their speeches. She renewed her vow to never set foot on Olympus or let the earth produce its fruits until she saw her daughter's face.

Zeus dispatched his chief messenger, Hermes, to the depths of the earth. Hermes found Hades on a couch with his pale and listless bride. "Hades!" said Hermes. "Zeus commands me to bring Persephone back to her mother. Demeter is planning to starve the mortals so to deprive the gods of their offerings!"

Hades would not openly disobey his brother's order. "Go, Persephone," he said. "Back to your mother!"

Joyously she sprang from the couch. Hades smiled grimly. "Before you go, dear wife, refresh yourself. You have eaten nothing while you have been here." He spread out seeds from a blood-red pomegranate, fruit of the dead. Persephone snatched four of the seeds as she leapt into the golden chariot. She swallowed them before she left the Kingdom of the Dead.

"She will return," said Hades.

Hermes drove out of the underworld to Eleusis where Demeter waited in her incense-filled temple. When she saw Persephone, she flew forward and clasped her daughter.

Demeter was suspicious that Hades had released this beautiful goddess. She gazed into Persephone's face and saw the stain of the pomegranate on her lips. "Did you eat anything in the underworld?" she asked.

"Yes, Mother!" said Persephone. "Before I left, Hades gave me pomegranate seeds."

"And you ate them?"

"Only four small seeds—he forced me," Persephone lied.

"My child, if you ate while you were in the Kingdom of the Dead, you can never completely leave. You must return to Hades for four months each year—one month for each seed," said Demeter. "But I swear while you are gone, no green shall grow. My tears will be cold rain. And when you come back to me, the earth will burst into flower, fruit, and grain."

At that moment, Zeus sent Rhea as a messenger. Rhea, who was mother to both Zeus and Demeter, said, "My daughter, Zeus wishes you to return to the company of the gods. Yield to him, lest you carry your anger too far. And bestow some nourishing fruit on mortal men!"

Demeter obeyed her mother. Immediately, the wide earth was weighed down with buds and blossoms. The brown Eleusinian plain transformed to fields of standing corn. Demeter returned to Olympus, crowned by a corn wreath, and took her rightful place among the gods.

Forever after, while Persephone was locked away in the underworld, Demeter withdrew her gifts; the earth was barren with winter. When they reunited, the goddess lavished her bounty, and spring returned on earth.

Elizabeth Morgan

1946-

On March 11, 1983, Dr. Elizabeth Morgan filed a petition for custody of her seven-month-old daughter Hilary. "I was a mother. A primeval urge told me to protect and love and fight and die for my child."[1] Briefly married to Hilary's father, Dr. Eric Foretich, she had separated from him before the baby was born.

Foretich fought for custody by declaring Elizabeth an unfit mother. Each parent marshaled teams of lawyers, psychiatrists, social workers, family, and friends. After a five-day trial in November 1985, the judge awarded custody to Morgan and overnight visitation rights to Foretich.

Morgan wrote about this legal struggle in *Custody: A True Story*. "Giving me [Hilary], whose rightful place was with me, was no cure for the scars left by the courtroom. I was afraid I had been destroyed, afraid that the system had given her to me after letting me be scarred, battered, broken, and rendered unfit to be a mother."[2]

Perhaps Morgan thought custody was a settled issue. However, custody is never settled while the child is under the age of majority; custody is always subject to change of circumstances.

The Morgan-Foretich battle reignited in 1985, when she accused him of sexually abusing their two-and-a-half-year-old daughter during visitation. He denied the allegation and accused her of mental illness. And thus both parents began anew the bitter custody battle that lasted years, involved Congress, and became publicized by the world press.

After investigations and a twelve-day hearing, District of Columbia Superior Court Judge Herbert Dixon, Jr. ruled that Morgan did not prove the sexual abuse. Morgan refused to turn her daughter over to Foretich for a court-ordered unsupervised two-week visit. Instead, she sent her parents into hiding with five-year-old Hilary. They disappeared from the Washington area in August 1987. When Judge Dixon asked Morgan where the child was, she answered, "I'm not going to tell you." He ordered her to the D.C. jail until she delivered Hilary for visitation.

For 759 days, she lived in a six-by-eleven-foot cell. On the cinderblock wall, she wrote in crayon, *Was mich nicht zugrunde richtet, macht mich starker.* ("What doesn't kill me outright makes me stronger.") She recalls:

> For the average middle-class American, living in the D.C. jail is a horror. It's dirty, it's noisy, it's crowded, and you have no privacy. But I chose this because the middle-class American existence is worthless to me if my daughter is being raped. The destruction of my child is not worth any possessions. Just having her safe makes me happy.[3]

Morgan challenged the constitutionality of her confinement. An unprecedented forty-nine motions, fifteen appeals, and four full oral arguments flooded the appellate court. On August 5, 1988, the D.C. Court of Appeals upheld Morgan's jailing for contempt. The court also commented on the tragedy of the custody suit:

> A Kikuyu proverb tells us: "When elephants fight, it is the grass that suffers." Here, the grass is a little girl who will be six years old this month. For almost a year, she has been deprived of the company of both father and mother. She is the principal figure in a drama of appalling proportions, no matter what the outcome.[4]

Publicity about Morgan's incarceration created support for her cause; *Glamour* and *People* magazines ran sympathetic articles. Frank Wolf, a Republican from Virginia, introduced a bill in the U.S. House of Representatives to limit the time a person can spend in jail on a contempt charge in a child-custody case in the District of Columbia to eighteen months. Congress passed the Morgan bill.[5]

On September 25, 1989, Morgan walked out of jail. Dressed in an orange jail jumpsuit and carrying a dozen yellow roses, she greeted her fiance, Paul Michel, a U.S. Court of Appeals judge. She said Hilary would remain in hiding. "The one thing I have learned in the two years I have kept her safe is that by giving no information I'm protecting her."[6]

In November 1989, ABC Broadcasting televised a docudrama about Morgan's jailing. Judge Dixon was portrayed as the intransigent villain ruling against an embattled mother. Also during December, Morgan wed Judge Paul Michel.

In the meantime, Morgan's parents, Antonia and William Morgan had fled with Hilary. For twenty-two months, they hid in Nassau, Toronto, Vancouver, Glasgow, England, Singapore, Auckland…They posed as a retired couple taking their granddaughter on a pleasure trip.

Finally, they took Hilary to New Zealand where the government had not signed the International Hague Convention of 1980. Therefore, the country was not legally required to return wrongfully abducted children to their country of origin. The couple rented a furnished apartment in a motel in Christchurch. Hilary attended a private elementary school and learned to ride a bike.

Foretich maintained his international search for Hilary. After receiving a tip, his private investigators found her in Christchurch in February 1990. The international press broke the news. Foretich and Morgan both flew to New Zealand to fight the custody battle. New Zealand maintained jurisdiction over the case and appointed neutral experts to examine Hilary and make recommendations to the court.

Morgan moved in with Hilary and her parents and prepared to become a permanent citizen. Pleading financial troubles, Foretich returned to the United States. He informed the court by affidavit that he would not contest the custody if Hilary remained in New Zealand.

In November 1990, the New Zealand family court awarded custody to Morgan on condition that Hilary remain in her school in Christchurch. The court did not hear evidence or rule on the charges of sexual abuse because the abuse had allegedly occurred six years earlier on another continent. The court-appointed psychiatrist said, "It is no longer possible to distinguish fact from belief."[7] However, Foretich was not allowed to visit, telephone, or send letters, because Hilary was deemed not psychologically ready for contact with her father.

After obtaining custody, Morgan settled in Christchurch with her mother and Hilary. Twice a year, Morgan's new husband visited from Washington D.C. Newspapers reported that Hilary was becoming a typical "kiwi" girl.[8]

In 1997, Congressman Wolf helped pass a second law that affected the custody suit. The "Morgan Bill" was an amendment to the federal transportation appropriation bill. The law removed Morgan's case from the U.S. courts and allowed her to return to the United States without losing her daughter or being punished for ignoring Judge Dixon's order.[9] Mother and daughter returned to the United States. Morgan declined to live in the District of Columbia, the jurisdiction of Judge Dixon.

In May 1997, Foretich filed a lawsuit against the United States, claiming Congress passed a law stripping his rights as a father. Because the bill was narrowly tailored to punish him and benefit Morgan, he alleged it was an unconstitutional bill of attainder. Foretich did not seek custody of his daughter; instead, he wanted to assure his daughter was safe and to clear his name of wrongdoing.[10]

REVIVING OUR PEOPLE

Women can help turn the world right side up.
—Wilma Mankiller

Spider Brings the Fire

Cherokee People

In the beginning there was no fire and the world was cold. The people longed for warmth and light on long, dark winter nights.

One night, the Thunders struck a sycamore tree with lightning. A fire started in the hollow. The tree stood on an island and the people could see the smoke and flames. They held a council to decide who would go and fetch the fire. Every animal that could fly or swim wanted to go.

Raven went because he was large and strong. He flew across the water and landed on the sycamore tree. Before he could decide how to retrieve the fire, the heat scorched him. He flew back without the fire, but his feathers were burned black.

Screech Owl said, "I will go." He flew to the island and looked down into the hollow tree. A blast of hot air shot up and burned his eyes. He flew away without the fire, but his eyes are red to this day.

Hunting Owl and Horned Owl went next. But the hot ashes flew into their eyes. They came back without the fire and with white circles around their eyes. No more birds volunteered to go.

Black Racer swam out to the sycamore tree. The heat burned his body black. Since that day, the snake darts back and forth as if trying to escape the burning tree.

When the animals refused to fetch the fire, Water Spider spoke up. "I will go."

The animals said, "Water Spider, you can run on top of the water to the island, but how will you bring back the fire?"

"I have a way," said Water Spider. She spun a thread and wove a *tusti* bowl. She fastened the bowl to her back and stepped out on the water. The animals saw her red stripes as she crossed to the island. Water Spider went to the burning tree and chose one small glowing ember. She put the ember in her spider-spun bowl and carried it back safely to the council of animals. She fanned that small ember into a blazing fire, which has warmed us all from that day to this.

Wilma Pearl Mankiller
1945-

Wilma Mankiller is the former Principal Chief of the Cherokee Nation of Oklahoma and the first female in modern history to lead a major Native American tribe. Her family name "Mankiller" is an old military title similar to "general." When someone jokes about her name, she resorts to humor. "I look the person in the eye and say with a straight face that Mankiller is actually a well-earned nickname. That usually shuts the person up."[1]

For her first eleven years, she grew up on Mankiller Flats, among a traditional Cherokee community. The land was deeded to her grandfather in 1907 when Oklahoma became a state. Her family of ten brothers and sisters, living without electricity and running water, lived self-sufficiently by hunting, bartering, and raising their own food. In 1956, drought forced her family to move to a San Francisco housing project as part of the federal Bureau of Indian Affairs' plan to relocate rural Native Americans to large cities and "mainstream" them into American culture.

Her interest in her heritage ignited in 1969 when she and a group of university students occupied Alcatraz Island to publicize issues affecting their tribes. Next, she worked in educational programs in the Pit River Tribe.

In 1977, after marriage and divorce, she returned with her two daughters to her ancestral land and immediately began full-time service to her people. Mankiller wanted to aid economic development. Helping establish the Cherokee Community Development Department, she believed that the best way was not through government handouts but through taking responsibility for their own changes. She said, "Native Americans can help themselves if given half a reasonable chance."[2]

One of her best accomplishments was the Bell Community Revitalization Project. The Cherokee community of Bell had 350 residents, many of whom lived in inadequate housing with no indoor plumbing. When Mankiller asked the community what they wanted, they replied, "Water and indoor plumbing." She promised to get the supplies and advice if they would help build the water system.

Because of a history of other broken promises, the residents were distrustful. Mankiller gained their trust by writing grant proposals for federal funds and soliciting donations and equipment from private sources. Men, women, and children kept their promise and joined in building the sixteen-mile water pipeline. The water project story appeared on *Sunday Morning,* a CBS television program.[3]

Bolstered by success and pride, the community tackled Bell's housing. Again, Mankiller worked to get federal funds and the people did the rebuilding. The community center and twenty houses were rehabilitated, and with funds from the Cherokee Housing Authority, residents built twenty-five new houses. Mankiller said the Bell Project validated her belief that the Cherokee people had a willingness to help each other. "I also knew we had the capacity to solve our own problems…"[4]

Two years after the Bell Project, Ross Swimmer, chief of the Cherokee Nation, asked Mankiller to run as his deputy chief. Initially, her candidacy was opposed because she was a woman. She received hate mail and threatening telephone messages. Her tires were slashed. But when the votes were tallied, Swimmer and Mankiller had won.

When Swimmer resigned in 1985 to head the Bureau of Indian Affairs, Mankiller assumed the duties of chief. In the historic tribal elections of 1987, Mankiller was officially elected to the position. In 1991, despite health problems, including a kidney transplant, she ran and was reelected to office with 82.7 percent of the vote. Six women were also elected to the fifteen-member tribal council.

Under her leadership, the Cherokee Nation revived. Tribal

membership increased by 100,000; the annual budget increased by $40 million. In 1990, she signed an agreement that the Cherokee Nation would administer federal funds instead of the Bureau of Indian Affairs. The tribe added three health centers and nine children's programs.[5]

In April 1994, in front of five hundred tribal employees, Mankiller cited a passage from the Book of Ecclesiastes: "To everything there is a season." Then she said, "My season here is coming to an end." She would not seek reelection. Vowing to stay active, she said, "You don't have to have a title or a position to be effective."[6] President Clinton awarded the Presidential Medal of Freedom, the nation's highest civilian honor, to Mankiller in January 1998.

DELIVERING OUR BABIES

There is a tender regard one woman bears to another, and a natural sympathy in those that have gone thro' the Pangs of Childbearing: which, doubtless, occasion a compassion for those that labour under these circumstances, which no man can be a judge of.
—eighteenth-century midwifery manual

The Fairies' Midwife

Scotland

In the days of long ago, an old woman lived in the wildest part of Scotland. She attended all the births in her district and many of the children were named after her.

One night she was having a doze by the fire when she was wakened by rapping on the door. Two wee men said, "Follow us; there's a bairn who needs your help to be born."

The midwife wrapped her cloak around her and followed them into the dark. They had a long trek before the men announced, "We're here." They took her inside a stately manor.

What a sight she saw! A great hall was lit by chandeliers. The furniture was made of gold and silver and studded with emeralds and rubies. The men took the midwife to a chamber draped with silk and lace. On the bed lay a beautiful lady. Her golden ringlets were wet from the strain of birthing her child.

The midwife went to her side and helped bring the baby into the world. "What a bonny boy!" said the old woman as she bathed and dressed the child.

"Anoint his eyes with this ointment," said the mother, handing a tin to the midwife. "Beware; don't get any in your own eyes."

The midwife put the ointment in the baby's eyes with her finger. Then her left eye began to itch, so she rubbed it with the same finger. Immediately, with her left eye, she saw the lavish room was merely a cave; the silken bed was a bundle of rushes. And the mother wasn't a grand lady at all; she was one of the serving maids who had disappeared from a nearby town.

The midwife shut her left eye and opened her right. Again she saw the fine room and lady. "They've cast a glamor over me!" she cried out. "Things are not as they seem!"

One of the men asked, "What do you see?"

"With one eye, a fine manor. With the other eye, a bare cave."

"I'll remedy that," said the man. He led the midwife to the door and pushed her outside. Before he shut the door, he blew on her eyes.

The midwife found herself standing alone on a moonlit moor. Gone were the manor, the cave, the mother, the bairn. And she never saw the fairies again.

Onnie Lee Logan
1910–1985

From the beginning of our country's history, women have supported one another emotionally and physically during childbirth; a midwife was among the Mayflower settlers. Until 1910, midwives delivered the majority of American babies.[1] By 1930, 80 percent of the practicing midwives were in the South, where "granny" midwives attended most of the births of low-income women.[2]

Onnie (pronounced "Ownee") Lee Logan was a "granny" midwife whose oral autobiography was recorded by Katherine Clark in the book *Motherwit*. Her story tells about her routine practices in midwifery and her extraordinary attitudes about life.

Logan was born around 1910 in Alabama, the fourteenth of sixteen children. She was delivered by a midwife. Her mother was a midwife and her grandmother, who had been a slave, had also been a midwife—unlicensed and unschooled as granny midwives were.

As Logan said, "Those old midwives in those days was black womens not doin it for a job but doin it as a person knowin there was need for it. They were doin the very best they could to help."[3] In 1919, Alabama began to regulate midwifery through the county boards of health.

Although Logan went to work as a maid for a doctor's family, her dream was to deliver babies. She said, "When I told Dr. Mears I wanted to be a midwife he thought it was a wonderful job."[4] She took a nine-month course with the board of health and got her permit in 1949.

While Logan was apprenticing with another midwife at a delivery, twins were born. The midwife could not get the firstborn to breathe. She lay the baby down and delivered the second baby. Logan picked up the first boy, who fit in the palm of her hand, and felt a faint, irregular heartbeat. She said, "I asked God to he'p me bring that baby to life if life was in it and He gave me power to do it." In spite of having no training in resuscitation, she instinctively blew in the baby's mouth and pumped on its stomach. After being worked on for forty-five minutes, he breathed and survived. Logan recounted in her book:

> There was a higher power and God gave me wisdom. Motherwit, common sense. Wisdom come from on high. You got it and you cain't explain how you got it yo'self. It's motherwit.[5]

According to the Alabama regulations at that time, pregnant women had to visit their physicians for prenatal care and for written permission to have home delivery. Logan made certain that her patients were examined by their doctors, then met with them three or four times before the delivery to make preparations.

When she went to a delivery, she dressed in a white cap and coat and carried a bag of sterilized equipment. Legally, she was not allowed to carry medicine. After scrubbing herself and preparing the birthing bed and equipment, Logan would stay with the laboring patient. She said doctors and nurses didn't have the time. "I'm with my patients at all times with a smile and keepin her feelin good with kind words."[6]

Logan, like most midwives, emphasized the normality of childbirth and provided supportive care with minimal intervention. "Childbirth is not a sickness," she said.[7] She kept her patients on their feet and helped them breathe to control the pain of contractions. And she waited for the birthing to proceed naturally. "You cain't hurry God. A midwife like me, they just take their time and let God work the plan."[8]

She delivered about one thousand babies. She also sewed baby clothes, supplied food to families, and cooked and cared for older children. Often she took payment in the form of homegrown vegetables.

Although the state of Alabama outlawed midwifery in 1976, Logan was allowed to continue assisting births. But in 1984, she received a letter telling her that her services were no longer needed and her permit would not be renewed.[9]

In 1989, her book *Motherwit* was published. In 1993, Katherine Clark fashioned a one-woman show from the book. The play *Motherwit* was performed by actress Tonea Stewart in Montgomery, Alabama. Onnie Lee Logan sat alone in the second row at the rehearsal, hearing her words spoken back to her.[10]

Logan's story is full of soul-shattering poverty, bigotry, long days as a maid, and long nights as a midwife. But the final words in her book tells how she viewed her life:

> I believe God pulled out all of his blessin's on me and I appreciate 'em and put 'em to good work. So I'm satisfied at what I've done…I was a good midwife. One of the best as they say. This book was the last thing I had planned to do until God said well done. I consider myself—in fact if I leave tomorrow—I've lived my life and I've lived it well.[11]

HEALING OUR SICK

I think of death as some delightful journey
That I shall take when all my tasks are done.
—Ella Wheeler Wilcox, "The Journey"

Godmother Death

Mexico

Long ago, a poor woman gave birth to a son. She wanted him baptized, but could find no one to be the godmother. She rocked her baby. "Don't worry, my child. I will ask the first woman I meet to be your *madrina.*"

She dressed her son in his finest garments and carried him to church. Along the roadside, she met a thin, old woman dressed in black. The mother approached her, "Señora, I am going to the church to baptize my son. Will you consent to be his madrina, por favor?"

"I would be honored," answered the old woman. She took the baby in her arms.

The mother guessed the old woman was an ordinary villager—but she was not. She was Death, *La Muerta*—the one who comes to take the souls away in her cart. At the baptism, Madrina Muerta promised to be a good guardian. Then she left.

Nine years later, on the day of the boy's first communion, the madrina came to the church. "I am your godmother," she said. "For your gift, I will make you a great healer, *el curandero.* I will come to you when you are older."

When the boy had grow to manhood, his godmother visited again. "Come with me, so I can explain how we will work together."

47

Madrina Muerta took her godson to her great house. She led him through hallways and rooms into the cavernous cellars. The cellars were lit by the flames of thousands upon thousands of burning candles, candles of every height and width. Some candles were newly lighted; some burned halfway; some were nearly extinguished.

Madrina Muerta pointed at the candles. "Each person has a candle, which I light at birth. When the candle burns out, it is time for me to collect their soul. Remember what you see."

She took him upstairs to the dining room where the table was laden with food and wine. After dining together, she said, "Son, this is how we can work together. You study herbs and learn to make cures. Then when you are called to the bedside of a sick person, look for me. If I am standing at the foot of the bed, it is a sign that the sick one will not die. Use your salves, teas, and packets of medicines: you will cure the illness. But if I am standing at the head of the bed, do not try your cures. I have come to take the sick one. You must look sad and say you cannot help. Do you understand?"

The godson nodded. "I understand and I will obey you."

Madrina Muerte raised her glass. "People will pay you much money for your cures and respect your wisdom when you predict death. Look for me at the bedside."

Before parting, she wiped her godson's ears with a magic salve. "Adios."

As the godson walked home, he heard herbs and flowers whispering in the fields. He picked up a leaf of basil. Softly it told him, *I cure colic.*

The desert lavender said, *I cure hangovers.*

The cat's claw said, *And I cure tumors.*

Each plant whispered its healing secrets, because the magic salve had opened his ears.

The godson spend his days learning the wisdom of the plants. He apprenticed himself to a curandero and learned what symptoms responded to his herbal remedies. At last, he was mature in years, skilled in medicine, and eager to begin his own practice.

Visiting the home of his first patient, he entered the sick room. Madrina Muerta stood at the foot of the bed. No one else could see her. The godson gave a nod of respect, then set about the work of easing the patient's pain. Because of his godmother's help, he was confident that his cure would succeed. The patient recovered.

More and more patients sought his care. His cures were miraculous, but he also knew when medicines were useless. He was careful not to try to save a patient when Madrina Muerte stood at the head of the sickbed. Soon he was a rich and famous curandero.

One day the king called him to heal the princess. "If you save her life, she will be your bride."

When the curandero entered the sickroom, he saw his godmother standing at the head of the bed. He nodded to her and prepared to tell the king that his medicines could not save the princess. But the princess was lovely; the curandero was eager to have her for his wife.

He called for servants. "Turn the bed around. Place the foot of the bed in the opposite direction."

The servants turned the bed, so Madrina Muerta was standing at the foot. The princess roused enough for the curandero to administer his cure. When she was restored to health, she consented to be his bride.

His godmother summoned him to her house. "Come. Let me reveal to you the consequences of your actions."

She beckoned him down into the cellars. Showing him to a tall, brightly burning candle, she said, "This was once your candle. But you disobeyed me and saved a life that was over. Even though you are my beloved godson, I cannot change what you have done. You have traded for the candle belonging to the princess."

She pointed to a small candle. It flickered, sputtered, and went out.

"Come, ride with me," the madrina said. When she came with her cart, he climbed inside. During the journey, he asked forgiveness for disobeying her. He thanked her for his life as a great curandero. As they talked about old times, he became drowsy and fell asleep on her lap. Madrina Muerte took her godson to eternity.

Teresa Urrea

1873–1906

A sixteen-year-old girl lay on a table, dressed in white, her hands folded across her chest and bound with blue ribbon. Candles burned at her head and feet. Her coffin stood open. Praying women knelt in the candlelight. Outside the hacienda, men warmed themselves at bonfires. "Teresita is with the angels now," the people said.[1]

The wake was for "Teresita," the affectionate nickname of Teresa Urrea. Teresa's mother, an unmarried fourteen-year-old, was a Yaqui Indian; her father was Don Tomas Urrea, an aristocratic rancher. For the early years of her life, Teresa lived with her mother in a dirt-floored hut. Then her father took her to his ranch in Cabona, located in the state of Sonora, Mexico.

Interested in healing, Teresa apprenticed herself to Huila, an old servant woman. Huila, a *curandera,* taught Teresa how to use herbal medicines. Huila nursed Teresa when the girl became gravely ill. A Mexican newspaper reported that when a suitor tried to rape the girl, she had a seizure and lapsed into a coma.[2]

Day after day, Teresa lay unconscious. Huila dared not give her charge herbal concoctions or even a sip of water for fear of choking her. She applied cool poultices to the girl's face, brushed her long hair, and said prayers at her bedside until the girl was pronounced dead.

During the night of the wake, the candle at Teresa's head flared. Teresa opened her eyes and sat up. A woman screamed; all mourners rushed from the room—except Huila. She did not move.

"What does this mean?" Teresa looked around the room.

"You were dead," said Huila. "But I prayed to the Blessed Virgin to bring you back."

Teresa said, "Yes, the Virgin was here; she told me of the many things I must do. She said I have special powers and must use them to cure people."

Don Tomas and the crowd rushed to see Teresa's miraculous return from the dead. "Prepare some broth," Don Tomas ordered, "and make it with bull's meat to give her strength."

Huila spooned the broth into the girl. Before Teresa fell asleep, she told the old woman, "Tell Papa I do not need my coffin, but save it. It will be used in three days."[3]

Three days later, Huila was found dead in her room; she had died quietly in her sleep. The old curandera was buried at the ranch cemetery in Teresa's coffin.

During the months after Huila's death, Teresa gradually

assumed the role of curandera. Word about the beautiful girl's healings spread. A steady stream of seekers came to the ranch, which became known as the "Lourdes of Mexico." They called Teresa "the Saint of Cabona."

The Mexican government was hostile to Teresa, fearing that she was a symbol for the rebellious peasants. She fled across the border. In the United States, thousands of people in Tucson, El Paso, and San Francisco sought her cures. At thirty-three, she died of consumption (pulmonary tuberculosis) and was buried beside her father in Clifton, Arizona. The cemetery is now a slag heap from smelted copper. Although her grave is gone, she is honored by the town's annual Fiesta de la Santa de Cabona.[4]

COMFORTING OUR GRIEVING

*All sorrows can be borne if you put them into
a story or tell a story about them.*
　　—Isak Dinesen

Beruriah's Jewels

Israel

One Sabbath, the celebrated Rabbi Meir was teaching at the yeshiva. His wife Beruriah was at home with their two sons. The boys fell ill with a fever and Beruriah summoned the physician. In spite of all his efforts, he could not save the boys. The boys died before nightfall.

Beruriah lay them on her marriage-bed and spread a white covering over them. She sat alone with them. "This is the Sabbath," she told herself. "I will not profane this holy day with weeping."

She put on her Sabbath clothes and waited for her husband's return. When he came, he asked, "Where are the boys?"

"You will see them soon," she replied.

When the sun set, Beruriah brought the lamp-wick and the spice box for the celebration of Habdalah. Rabbi Meir filled the wine cup. "Where are my sons? I want them to drink from the cup of blessing."

His wife reassured him, "They are not far off."

The rabbi pronounced the blessing that separated the day of rest from the days of work; the Sabbath was over. They ate the evening meal.

When they had finished eating, Beruriah said, "Husband, please advise me on a difficult matter. Some years ago, a rich traveler came to our house. He knew your reputation as an honest man. He gave me some jewels to safeguard for him. That traveler has come again; he claims his jewels."

The rabbi said, "I am surprised to learn of these happenings, but what advice do you want?"

"Husband," said Beruriah, "I have come to prize these precious jewels. Must I give them back?"

"My wife, you are a woman of virtue and wisdom; you know the answer. The traveler has honored us with his trust. Return the jewels cheerfully."

"Dear husband," said Beruriah softly, "Remember your words."

She took him by the hand and led him to the bed where the boys lay. She drew back the cover. "These are all the jewels of which I can boast," she said.

Together they wept and lamented and comforted each other until at last they proclaimed, "The Lord gave, the Lord has taken away, and blessed be the name of the Lord!"

Rose Fitzgerald Kennedy
1890–1995

On Friday, November 22, 1963, Rose Kennedy was at Hyannisport, Massachusetts, anticipating the annual family Thanksgiving dinner. In the morning, she went to mass, played nine holes of golf, and ate lunch with her husband. While preparing for an afternoon nap, she was told that her son, President John F. Kennedy, had been shot. Soon after, news came of his death. In her autobiography, she wrote, "I had trained myself through the years not to become too visibly upset at bad news, even very bad news, because I had a strong notion that if I broke down, everybody else in the household would."[1]

Rose Kennedy spent the afternoon walking on the beach and asking, *Why?* She said: "My reaction to grief takes in part the form of nervous activity. I have to keep moving, walking, pulling away at things, praying to myself as I move, and making up my mind that I am not going to be defeated by tragedy. Because there are the living still to work for, while mourning for the dead."[2]

Having adopted a habit that bad news should be faced in the morning, not at night, she decided to conceal the tragedy from her husband until the next morning. The Kennedy patriarch was bedridden from a stroke, unable to speak or move his right arm or leg. She called their children and doctor to come to his bedside. The next day, after attending mass with his mother, Ted Kennedy broke the news to his father.

Rose Kennedy was present at all funeral ceremonies. Joining the thousands of mourners at the Capitol rotunda, she visited the flag-draped coffin. She attended the funeral at St. Matthew's Cathedral. She stood beside the burial plot at Arlington National Cemetery while Air Force One flew overhead. She accepted condolences at the White House from world dignitaries. Then she went home to sit at her husband's side.

Continuing her life, Rose Kennedy cared for Joe Kennedy, attended mass, played golf, and visited with her family. At seventy-seven years of age, she went on the campaign trail when her son Bobby Kennedy decided to run for the presidency.

On June 4, 1968, she went to sleep in Hyannisport after hearing that Bobby was ahead in the California presidential primary. She woke the next morning and heard on the television that her son had been shot in the head. She said, "It seemed impossible that the same kind of disaster could befall our family twice in five years."[3] She went to mass and said later, "I really don't remember what was said or much of what I was thinking, except that I was praying, 'Lord have mercy!' and thinking, 'Oh, Bobby, Bobby, Bobby.'"[4]

The following day, Bobby Kennedy died. His body was flown to New York City, lain in state in St. Patrick's Cathedral, and was taken by train for burial in Washington, D.C. On board the train, Rose Kennedy encouraged her children and grandchildren to wave to the grieving crowds lining the tracks. She said, "If people cared enough to come out and pay their respects we ought at least to give them some sign of appreciation."[5]

Because the family received so many messages of sympathy, Rose Kennedy decided to express her gratitude on television. She also explained her view of the tragedies:

> We cannot always understand the ways of Almighty God. The crosses which He Sends us, the sacrifices which He demands of us...But we accept with faith and resignation His Holy Will, with no looking back to what might have been, and we are at peace.[6]

After John's assassination, Joe Kennedy had given up trying to recuperate from his stroke. After Bobby's assassination, he rapidly declined. He died on November 18, 1969, with Rose Kennedy kneeling at his bedside.

The matriarch of the Kennedy clan remained active until she suffered a stroke in 1984. For her motto, she adapted words from John Buchan's *Pilgrim's Way*, "I know not age, nor weariness nor defeat."[7]

She died at age 104, leaving five children, twenty-eight grandchildren, and forty-one great-grandchildren. Teddy Kennedy said, "She had a long and extraordinary life, and we loved her deeply. She was the most beautiful rose of all."[8]

PERFORMING MIRACLES

Miracles happen only to those who believe in them.

—French proverb

Saint Brigid's Cloak

Ireland

So it is said that Saint Brigid was the Abbess of Kildare who did great charitable works. When she wanted some land in Leinster to build a church, she took her nuns to the king's castle. The king was away hunting, so Saint Brigid waited by the gate. When the king rode up, he saw a blue flag waving. It wasn't a flag at all; it was Saint Brigid's cloak fluttering in the wind.

The tight-pursed king guessed that she was there for money for her charities. He cut her greetings short: "Don't be flying your cloak like a flag in front of my castle. I've neither silver nor gold to give you."

"It's not money I'm begging," Saint Brigid assured him, "just a wee bit of ground for a church."

"Bride of Kildare," the King of Leinster said, "where would I be getting this ground? I've none to spare."

"Just the barest bit of rock will do," she replied. "At least grant me as much land as my cloak will cover."

The king thought, *She'll wheedle me to death. I'd best give her what she wants.* He said, "Just what your cloak will cover. Not an inch more."

At that, Saint Brigid lifted her cloak to catch the wind. "Away with it," she called to her nuns. Four sisters caught the hem of the cloak and ran in the four directions of the compass. The cloak billowed

57

and expanded. More sisters picked up the cloak and ran and ran until it covered almost a mile in every direction.

"Stop!" cried the king, for it seemed that her blue cloak would cover the whole of Leinster.

Stop she did—when she was ready and when she was sure the king was convinced of her power. Of all the land her cloak had covered, Saint Brigid claimed only a few rocky acres to build a church. And afterward, she only had to mention her miraculous cloak for the king to freely open his purse to her charities.

Saint Frances Xavier Cabrini
1850–1917

Saint Frances Xavier Cabrini, the first American saint, once said, "Like Saint Teresa, with five pennies and God, I can accomplish many great things."[1] Many great things she did accomplish—the establishment of orphanages, hospitals, and convents on three continents.

Francesca Maria Cabrini was born in Italy in 1850, the youngest of thirteen children. Religious from early childhood, she dreamed of becoming a missionary. Six years after taking her final vows as a nun, she founded the Missionary Sisters of the Sacred Heart.

In 1889, under the instructions of Pope Leo XIII, she and six other nuns sailed to New York City to help the Italian immigrants. In the following years, Mother Cabrini built schools in New York, New Orleans, Chicago, Denver, Seattle, and Los Angeles. In 1910, she became a naturalized United States citizen.

The frail, petite nun with luminous eyes was a gifted fund-raiser, as evidenced by an incident that occurred in Seattle in 1912. The existing Seattle orphanage was in the path of a highway expansion. Mother Cabrini set out on foot to find a new location; she found nothing.

Then one night, she dreamed of a villa on a hill. The next morning, she took a map and put her finger on a location. She told the sisters, "Go there and report about your findings."

The nuns obeyed, although they doubted they would find anything suitable. But when they returned they said, "Oh, Mother, we went exactly where you told us to go, and found a little paradise on earth."

Mother Cabrini and the nuns walked to the villa on the hill. A man told them the estate belonged to his wife and she would not part with it for all the gold on earth. As they left, Mother Cabrini said the paradise would be for the orphans, "somehow or another."

The exhausted women began the long walk back to the convent. When Mother Cabrini saw a limousine pass, she hailed it and was offered a drive by the woman passenger. Mother Cabrini talked about her dream for the villa. The woman discovered that the small nun was the famous Mother Cabrini and the villa she was discussing was her own home.

The woman said, "Mother Cabrini, the paradise you speak of is mine. I never thought of parting with it. But if I may be allowed to enter your holy house for just a moment and receive from your hands a glass of water in the name of Our Lord, your little orphans shall have their 'paradise' with all my heart."

Later Mother Cabrini would say that she had acquired the property with three treasures: "my love, a dream, and a glass of water in His name."[2]

Mother Cabrini died in 1917 and was beatified in 1938. Eight years later, in 1946, she became the first American saint—the patron saint of immigrants.

TEACHING
OUR CHILDREN

A life is not important except in the impact it has on other lives.
  —Jackie Robinson

Most Honored

United States

Not so long ago, in a small town, the town council decided to honor the most prominent citizen. "We'll give an award at the town's Fourth of July picnic."

"Who should we choose?" they asked.

The first council member said, "We should honor the richest man in town; he built the new library."

The second council member said, "We should honor our doctor. She has saved many lives."

The third council member said, "We should honor our judge. He has settled many cases with fairness."

The mayor said, "Invite all the candidates to the picnic. Let the people choose."

The town newspaper published the news that the most prominent citizen would be honored. It was the talk of the town. Who would it be—the rich man, the doctor, or the judge? "It's a hard choice," everyone agreed.

On the evening of the Fourth of July, people came to the square in the center of town, carrying picnic baskets full of fried chicken and cherry pies. The band played marches while the children chased fireflies and lit sparklers.

At last, the major climbed the stairs of the band pavilion. "Welcome to everyone," he called out. "We are here to celebrate our country's birthday with music and fireworks. We are also here to select our town's most prominent citizen. Please bring the candidates forward."

The richest man in town was brought forward. Everyone applauded; he had given money for the new library.

The doctor was brought forward. Everyone applauded; she had saved many lives.

The judge was brought forward. Everyone applauded; he had settled many cases with fairness.

Then a child's voice called out, "I have someone!"

The crowd parted as a boy led a white-haired woman up to the pavilion.

The boy turned and announced to everyone, "Here is my teacher. She's a good teacher and should be honored."

Surprised, the crowd was quiet, until a man shouted, "She was my teacher too!" Someone else added, "She taught me all I know."

The teacher had instructed almost everyone in the town—including the rich man, the doctor, and the judge. People began to applaud, whistle, and cheer; their choice was clear. The mayor came down and escorted the woman up the stairs, so the town could honor their most prominent citizen—their teacher.

Mary McLeod Bethune

1875–1955

Mary McLeod Bethune's life began on July 10, 1875, when she was born to freed slaves. She was the fifteenth of seventeen children; she was the first born free. Her mother continued to work for the former owner in exchange for five acres of land near Mayesville, South Carolina. Her father and brothers built a cabin on the land and the family grew vegetables and cultivated cotton.

Young Mary worked in the cotton fields, but she wanted to learn to read and write. Miss Emma Wilson had started a mission school for African-American children at the Trinity Presbyterian Church in Mayesville, and for the first time black children had a chance to get an education. At seven years of age, Mary became the first member of her family to go to school. She completed the sixth grade at the mission school.

As an outstanding student, she received a scholarship to attend Scotia Seminary near Concord, North Carolina. The scholarship was sponsored by a stranger, Mary Chrissman, a Quaker dressmaker from Colorado. Mary McLeod was twelve years old when she left home; she would not return for seven years.

Upon graduation from Scotia Seminary in 1894, Mary McLeod received another scholarship from Mary Chrissman to Dwight Moody's Institute for Home and Foreign Missions in Chicago. She dreamed of going to Africa, but was told that there were "no openings for a Negro missionary in Africa."[1]

She returned to Mayesville as a teaching assistant at the Presbyterian mission school. She became a missionary in her own country; she taught in Augusta, Georgia, Sumter, South Carolina, and Palatka, Florida. She married another teacher, Albertus Bethune and had a son, Albert ("Bert"). She eventually divorced her husband because he objected to her teaching, but she continued to be addressed as "Mrs. Bethune."

In 1904, she moved to Daytona, Florida, which had no school for blacks and where the living conditions were deplorable for the families of the men building the railroad. With a dollar and a half, Mrs. Bethune opened the Daytona Literary and Industrial School for Training Negro Girls. She held classes in a borrowed, run-down, four-room cottage near the railroad tracks in Daytona Beach's "Colored Town." She used boxes for chairs and mashed elderberries for ink. Her little boy and five girls were the first students.

Within two years, she had enrolled 250 students and needed a bigger building. Mrs. Bethune bought "Hell's Hole," a swampy garbage dump, with a down payment of fifteen dollars—pennies, nickels, and dimes wrapped in a handkerchief. On weekends, she rode her bike into Daytona to knock on doors for donations.

With the help of wealthy benefactors, she built a four-story building. She called it Faith Hall, because faith had built it. Over the front entrance were engraved the words ENTER TO LEARN. A second inscription inside the portal read DEPART TO SERVE. Within a decade, the school offered a high school education, with training in home economics, teaching, and nursing. The school outgrew Faith Hall, and in 1916, White Hall, a Georgian Revival–style brick building, was constructed, and the school renamed the Daytona Normal and Industrial Institute.

In 1923, because of financial problems, Mrs. Bethune merged her school with Cookman Institute, an all-boys school. With an enrollment that grew to 1600, Bethune-Cookman Institute was a grade school, high school, and college (which later became Bethune-Cookman College). Mary McLeod Bethune, speaking as the school's first president, said, "When I walk through the campus, with its stately palms and well-kept lawns, and think back to the dump heap foundation, I rub my eyes and pinch myself. And I remember my childish visions in the cotton fields."[2]

Mary McLeod Bethune became a national leader in education, child welfare, and civil rights: she led a drive to register black voters, she created the National Council of Negro Women to combat school segregation and the lack of health facilities among black children, and she was president of the prestigious National Association of Colored Women's clubs (NACW). She was a friend of Eleanor Roosevelt and was appointed by Franklin D. Roosevelt to direct the Negro Affairs Division of the National Youth Administration, which provided job training during the Great Depression.

When she lectured across America, she spoke of a "people garden": although, she said, people were like flowers—red, yellow, growing in a garden together—she knew of no black flower to make the analogy complete. Years later, in Switzerland, she discovered the black rose and ordered seventy-two black rosebushes planted at Bethune-Cookman College. She became known as the "Black Rose."[3]

On May 18, 1955, Bethune died of a heart attack. Her home, "The Retreat," on the campus of Bethune-Cookman College became a National Historic Landmark.

In the nation's capital, in Lincoln Park, a seventeen-foot bronze statue of Bethune was dedicated on the ninety-ninth anniversary of her birth. She is reaching out to hand her legacy to two children. The words of her last will and testament are inscribed on the base of the monument:

> I leave you love.
> I leave you hope.
> I leave you racial dignity...[4]

GIVING BIRTH
IN OLD AGE

*I do not know how you appeared in my womb;
it was not I who endowed you with breath and
life, I had not the shaping of your every part.
It is the creator of the world, ordaining the
process of man's birth and presiding over the
origin of things...*
—2 Maccabees 7:22-23

Elisabeth, Mother of John the Baptist
Bible

There was in the days of Herod, the king of Judaea, a certain priest named Zacharias, of the course of Abia: and his wife was of the daughters of Aaron, and her name was Elisabeth.

And they were both righteous before God, walking in all the commandments and ordinances of the Lord blameless.

And they had no child, because that Elisabeth was barren, and they both were now well stricken in years.

And it came to pass, that while he executed the priest's office before God in the order of his course,

According to the custom of the priest's office, his lot was to burn incense when he went into the temple of the Lord.

And the whole multitude of the people were praying without at the time of incense.

And there appeared unto him an angel of the Lord standing on the right side of the altar of incense.

And when Zacharias saw him, he was troubled, and fear fell upon him.

But the angel said unto him, Fear not, Zacharias: for thy prayer is heard; and thy wife Elisabeth shall bear thee a son, and thou shalt call his name John.

And thou shalt have joy and gladness; and many shall rejoice at his birth.

For he shall be great in the sight of the Lord, and shall drink neither wine nor strong drink; and he shall be filled with the Holy Ghost, even from his mother's womb.

And many of the children of Israel shall he turn to the Lord their God.

And he shall go before him in the spirit and power of Elias, to turn the hearts of the fathers to the children, and the disobedient to the wisdom of the just; to make ready a people prepared for the Lord.

And Zacharias said unto the angel, Whereby shall I know this? for I am an old man, and my wife well stricken in years.

And the angel answering said unto him, I am Gabriel, that stand in the presence of God; and am sent to speak unto thee, and to show thee these glad tidings.

And, behold, thou shalt be dumb, and not able to speak, until the day that these things shall be performed, because thou believest not my words, which shall be fulfilled in their season.

And the people waited for Zacharias, and marvelled that he tarried so long in the temple.

And when he came out, he could not speak unto them: and they perceived that he had seen a vision in the temple: for he beckoned unto them, and remained speechless.

And it came to pass, that, as soon as the days of his ministration were accomplished, he departed to his own house.

And after those days his wife Elisabeth conceived, and hid herself five months, saying,

Thus hath the Lord dealt with me in the days wherein he looked on me, to take away my reproach among men.

And in the sixth month the angel Gabriel was sent from God unto a city of Galilee, named Nazareth,

To a virgin espoused to a man whose name was Joseph, of the house of David; and the virgin's name was Mary.

And the angel came in unto her, and said, Hail, thou that art highly favoured, the Lord is with thee: blessed art thou among women.

And when she saw him, she was troubled at his saying, and cast in her mind what manner of salutation this should be.

And the angel said unto her, Fear not, Mary: for thou hast found favour with God.

And, behold, thou shalt conceive in thy womb, and bring

forth a son, and shalt call his name JESUS.

He shall be great, and shall be called the Son of the Highest: and the Lord God shall give unto him the throne of his father David:

And he shall reign over the house of Jacob for ever; and of his kingdom there shall be no end.

Then said Mary unto the angel, How shall this be, seeing I know not a man?

And the angel answered and said unto her, The Holy Ghost shall come upon thee, and the power of the Highest shall overshadow thee: therefore also that holy thing which shall be born of thee shall be called the Son of God.

And, behold, thy cousin Elisabeth, she hath also conceived a son in her old age: and this is the sixth month with her, who was called barren.

For with God nothing shall be impossible.

And Mary said, Behold the handmaid of the Lord; be it unto me according to thy word. And the angel departed from her.

And Mary arose in those days, and went into the hill country with haste, into a city of Judah;

And entered into the house of Zacharias, and saluted Elisabeth.

And it came to pass, that, when Elisabeth heard the salutation of Mary, the babe leaped in her womb; and Elisabeth was filled with the Holy Ghost:

And she spake out with a loud voice, and said, Blessed art thou among women, and blessed is the fruit of thy womb.

And whence is this to me, that the mother of my Lord should come to me?

For, lo, as soon as the voice of thy salutation sounded in mine ears, the babe leaped in my womb for joy.

And blessed is she that believed: for there shall be a performance of those things which were told her from the Lord.

And Mary said, My soul doth magnify the Lord,

And my spirit hath rejoiced in God my Saviour.

For he hath regarded the low estate of his handmaiden: for, behold, from henceforth all generations shall call me blessed.

For he that is mighty hath done to me great things; and holy is his name.

And his mercy is on them that fear him from generation to generation.

He hath shown strength with his arm; he hath scattered the proud in the imagination of their hearts.

He hath put down the mighty from their seats, and exalted them of low degree.

He hath filled the hungry with good things; and the rich he hath sent empty away.

He hath helped his servant Israel, in remembrance of his mercy;

As he spake to our fathers, to Abraham, and to his seed for ever

And Mary abode with her about three months, and returned to her own house.

Now Elisabeth's full time came that she should be delivered; and she brought forth a son.

And her neighbours and her cousins heard how the Lord had shown great mercy upon her; and they rejoiced with her.

And it came to pass, that on the eighth day they came to circumcise the child; and they called him Zacharias, after the name of his father.

And his mother answered and said, Not so; but he shall be called John.

And they said unto her, There is none of thy kindred that is called by this name.

And they made signs to his father, how he would have him called.

And he asked for a writing table, and wrote, saying, His name is John. And they marvelled all.

And his mouth was opened immediately, and his tongue loosed, and he spake, and praised God.

And fear came on all that dwelt round about them: and all these sayings were noised abroad throughout all the hill country of Judaea.

And all they that heard them laid them up in their hearts, saying, What manner of child shall this be! And the hand of the Lord was with him.

And his father Zacharias was filled with the Holy Ghost, and prophesied, saying,

Blessed be the Lord God of Israel; for he hath visited and redeemed his people,

And hath raised up an horn of salvation for us in the house of his servant David;

As he spake by the mouth of his holy prophets, which have been since the world began:

That we should be saved from our enemies, and from the hand of all that hate us;

To perform the mercy promised to our fathers, and to remember his holy covenant;

The oath which he sware to our father Abraham,

That he would grant unto us, that we being delivered out of the hand of our enemies might serve him without fear,

In holiness and righteousness before him, all the days of our life.

And thou, child, shalt be called the prophet of the Highest: for thou shalt go before the face of the Lord to prepare his ways;

To give knowledge of salvation unto his people by the remission of their sins,

Through the tender mercy of our God; whereby the dayspring from on high hath visited us,

To give light to them that sit in darkness and in the shadow of death, to guide our feet into the way of peace.

And the child grew, and waxed strong in spirit, and was in the deserts till the day of his showing unto Israel.

Arlette Schweitzer

1949–

While every birth is a miracle, some are miraculous enough to be recorded for history. The births of John the Baptist and Jesus were religious miracles recorded in the Bible. The births of Arlette Schweitzer's twin grandchildren were medical miracles recorded by television, newspapers, and magazines. Arlette Schweitzer gave birth to her own grandchildren.

Raised in South Dakota, she married Dan Schweitzer at fifteen years of age. They had two children, a son and a daughter, Christa. Arlette Schweitzer returned to school and became a school librarian.

When Christa was fourteen, the doctors discovered she had been born without a uterus; she would never bear children. Even at that age Christa was devastated. Arlette Schweitzer recalled, "When Christa was just a little girl, all she could talk about was becoming a mother."[1]

Christa graduated from high school and married Kevin Uchytil; they wanted children. Arlette Schweitzer said, "She was born without a uterus. I was young enough to lend her mine."[2] Fifteen months after the wedding, mother and daughter began treatment at the University of Minnesota Hospital. Arlette Schweitzer, who was going into menopause, needed hormone treatment to match her cycles to Christa's.[3]

On February 21, 1991, eleven of Christa's eggs were extracted and put in a petri dish with Kevin's sperm. Arlette Schweitzer was implanted with four fertilized eggs. Ten days later, mother called daughter. "Congratulations! You're pregnant."[4] The first ultrasound showed two tiny fetuses, no bigger than a "grain of rice."

On October 12, 1991, while watching a football game on television, Arlette Schweitzer's water broke. She went into labor and, with Christa at her side, had a caesarean section. Chad Daniel was delivered first, weighing six pounds, three ounces. Chelsea Arlette was delivered a few minutes later at four pounds, seven ounces.

While the babies were being tended by the medical staff, Arlette Schweitzer told her daughter, "I'm fine. Mommy, go see your babies." Christa inspected the newborns, kissing them and rubbing their feet. "I'll never forget the incredible love on her face," said her mother.[5]

Grandmother Arlette had no regret about her decision to carry her grandchildren. "I felt honored and blessed to be able to do this. As a devout Catholic, she said, "We believe this was part of God's plans for our lives."[6]

LOVING OUR STEPCHILDREN

Bind us together, Lord,
Bind us together with love.
—African-American Spiritual

The Lion's Whiskers

Ethiopia

Bizunesh, a woman from the Ethiopian highlands, married a traveling merchant from the lowlands. She left her family's stone house on a cool and dry plateau and went to live in her husband's round mud house on the hot and dry grasslands.

Bizunesh became the stepmother to Segab, a small boy with sad brown eyes. "I have always wanted a son," she said, hugging him. "I will try to be a good mother to you."

Segab pulled away from her. "Don't touch me. You are not my real mother. My mother is dead."

Soon, her husband went to sell goods in distant lands and Bizunesh was left to tend her stepson. The boy played hard every day, running through the bushes and tearing his garment. In the evening, she would mend his *shamma*. "Please, don't run in the bushes and tear your clothes."

Every day he waded in the river, soaking his shoes. Every evening she would dry them. "Please, don't wade in the river and ruin your shoes."

She saved him the choicest pieces of goat from the stew. "Please, eat just a little bit for me." He fed the food to the dog. He did not thank her for her kindnesses; he did not even speak to her.

One morning, Bizunesh woke and found Segab's bed empty. The boy stayed away all day and did not return at nightfall. Bizunesh cried herself to sleep. The next morning, after she searched for her stepson, she went to the house of the wise woman of the village. Bizunesh asked, "Do you know where Segab is?"

The wise woman shook her head. "I don't know where he is, but I do know something that will help you."

Bizunesh eyes brightened. "Tell me: I will do anything to win his love."

The wise woman said, "I will make you a magic charm, but first, you must bring me an important ingredient—three whiskers from the chin of a lion."

"Three whiskers from a lion's chin? How?" said Bizunesh. "I'll be killed."

The old woman waved Bizunesh away. "If you want the charm, you will find a way."

Because Bizunesh wanted peace in the house, she decided to find a way. She went to the river and scanned the horizon. Far away, she saw a lion sleeping in the sun. When Bizunesh crossed the river, the lion stood and roared a warning. It was a young male, a nomad, his ruff not fully grown. Bizunesh retreated back across the river. That night, when Segab did not return home for his meal, she did not eat either.

The next day, she waded the river, carrying some goat stew. She placed the meat on a rock near the bank. Bizunesh crossed back and watched while the lion came and swallowed huge chunks without chewing.

The following day, she crossed the river again and walked several hundred yards closer to the lion before she left the meat on a rock. She backed off when the lion came to eat. The fourth day, Bizunesh crossed the river and approached the lion by several hundred more yards before she left the meat. This time she stayed closer while he ate. Each night, she waited for her stepson's return. Each day, she urged herself to go closer to the lion.

As time went by, Bizunesh patiently advanced on the lion. At last, she placed the meat at his feet and he ate it. She stood by. After the meal, the lion groomed his face and paws and fell asleep. Bizunesh reached out and pulled three whiskers from his chin. The lion continued sleeping. Bizunesh ran back across the grassland, across the river to the wise woman's house.

"I have them! I have the three whiskers!" She held out her hand.

"Please make the charm so Segab will love me like a mother."

"There is no such magic charm," said the wise woman. "The magic is in the lessons you learned in getting close to the lion. If you got near enough to the lion to pluck three whiskers, you can get close to Segab."

Bizunesh went home with new wisdom and new determination. The next day, she carried food outside the village. When she caught sight of her stepson hiding behind an acacia tree, she put the food down and left. As she walked away, she glanced over her shoulder and saw the boy coming to the food and gobbling it up.

On the following day, Bizunesh left the food several hundred yards closer to their house. She again backed off when Segab came to eat. As days went by, she put the food in the yard, then just outside the door.

At last, she placed the meal just inside the door. She made no comment when Segab reached inside, grabbed the food, and ran.

Patiently, Bizunesh set out food for the boy. Day by day, Segab came in the house to grab the food. Gradually, he stayed longer, and soon he began sitting with Bizunesh to eat. Gradually, he began speaking to his stepmother. She remained quiet and listened to him.

One evening, as he watched her pour batter on the griddle, Segab asked her about the highlands. As they dipped the *injera* into the stew and ate their meal, she told him about her childhood in the mountains.

Another evening, he fingered his dirty, torn clothes. "My father is coming home soon. Can you help me look good when he returns?" Bizunesh sewed a new *shamma* and trimmed the border with beads; she helped him make new shoes.

On the day of the homecoming, Bizunesh and Segab stood outside the house, dressed in finery. Segab slipped his hand into his stepmother's hand and together they waited. Soon Bizunesh's husband came into to sight, walking beside his mule. She gave the boy a small nudge. "Run, little lion, run to your father."

Sarah Bush Johnston Lincoln

1788–1869

Ten-year-old Abe Lincoln and his twelve-year-old sister, Sarah, were alone in the Indiana woods. Their mother, Nancy Hanks Lincoln, was dead; their father, Thomas Lincoln, had gone back to Kentucky to find another wife. After six months, the "children had given him up as having been killed by some wild animal."[1] They lacked proper food and clothes, but Sarah cooked and cared for her brother as well as she could. At last their father returned in a wagon drawn by four horses. Out of the wagon stepped a large-boned woman with a kindly face. "Here's your new mammy," said Thomas.[2] How would the young Abe react to a replacement for his "angel mother"?

Only three years earlier, in 1816, the Lincoln family—Thomas, Nancy Hanks, Sarah, and Abraham—had set out from Kentucky to settle 160 acres near Little Pigeon Creek in the new state of Indiana. Thomas Lincoln cleared the land, planted the first crops, and raised a one-room cabin, eighteen feet square. For two years, the family eked out a sparse living. After working long hours, Nancy Hanks Lincoln taught Abraham and Sarah from *Dilworth's Speller*, a combination speller, grammar book, prayer book, and reader. They read and recited verses from the Bible. She told Bible stories, Indian tales, and hunting yarns.

In 1818, Nancy Hanks Lincoln died of the "milk sickness," a poisoning from drinking milk from cows that had eaten white snakeroot. Her final words to her son were reported as, "I am going away from you, Abraham, and I shall not return. I know that you will be a good boy and that you will be kind to Sarah and to your father. I want you to live as I taught you, and to love your Heavenly Father."[3] William H. Herndon, Abraham Lincoln's law partner, described her death as he had heard about it:

> She had done her work in this world. Stoop-shouldered, thin-breasted, sad—at times miserable—groping through the per-plexities of life, without prospect of any betterment in her condition, she passed from earth, little dreaming of the grand future that lay in store for the ragged, hapless little boy who stood at her bedside in the last days of her life.[4]

During his return to Kentucky, Thomas hastily courted and wed widow Sally Bush Johnston, an acquaintance of his youth. He borrowed a four-horse team to carry his tall bride, her three children, and her household goods back to Little Pigeon Creek.

The new wife and stepmother made a home out of the rundown cabin. She cleaned and repaired the dwelling; she spurred Thomas to lay a floor, put in windows and doors, and fill the cracks between the logs. Her furniture filled the house; Abraham had a feather bed and pillow for his loft. Sally made a linsey-woolsey shirt to replace his worn, outgrown deerskin shirt. "She soaped, rubbed, and washed the children clean, so that they looked pretty, neat, well, and clean. She sewed and mended their clothes and the children once more looked human as their own good mother left them."[5]

Although she could not read, Sally Bush brought books among her household goods: *Webster's Speller, Robinson Crusoe, Aesop's Fables.* She observed that Abe "read every book he could lay his hands on."[6] She insisted all the children go to school whenever a roving teacher was in the neighborhood.

Sally blended the two families and treated the children impartially. One of her children later reported, "When father and mother married he had children and we went there to live with her, and she took the children and mixed us all up together like hasty pudding, and has not known us apart since."[7]

Sally said of Lincoln as a boy, "His mind and mine, what little I had, seemed to run together, move in the same channel."[8] Stepmother and stepson also shared a sense of humor. Lincoln returned her love and called her Mama.

When Abe grew up, left home, and began to earn money, he sent a portion to his stepmother. As long as he lived, he helped provide for her comfort. She died in 1869, eight miles south of Charleston, Illinois, on the farm Abe helped purchase for her.[9]

SEEKING JUSTICE

*Fight, fight, fight everlastingly, not with your
claws and fists, but with your wits.*
—Belva Lockwood

The Lady and the Unjust Judge

Turkey

Now it came to pass that a certain *chöpdji,* or dust collector,
came to the city, worked, and saved five hundred piasters. He
planned to return to his village and family when he earned a little
more. In the meantime, he was afraid the money might be stolen. *I
will leave it with the cadi,* he thought. *Surely he can be trusted to
keep my money.*

Going to the *cadi,* he said, "Oh learned judge, with the help of
Allah, I have worked five years and saved a sum of five hundred
piasters. I need a safe place to leave it. Will you grant a boon to your
humble servant? Will you keep this money for me until I am ready
to return to my family?"

The cadi replied, "My son, I swear that this money will be kept
faithfully and returned when you ask for it."

The chöpdji departed, well satisfied.

Several days later, he heard that some travelers were going to his
village. "I am lonesome for my family; I'll take what savings I have
and go home."

He went to the cadi. "Esteemed judge, I have come for my
money."

"What money?" the cadi replied, ringing a bell. Six guards
rushed in and threw the dust collector into the street—brooms,
brushes, and all.

He sat outside and wept. "It's so unfair," he said. "But I have no receipt. Who will believe the word of a chöpdji against the word of the great cadi?"

But someone did believe him. The very next day, he was sweeping the refuse from the home of a wealthy woman. His soul uttered such a sigh that she asked what troubled him. He told her about the unjust judge.

The lady, who was as kind as she was rich, thought for a few minutes. She told him, "Tomorrow at noon, I will visit the cadi. Wait a few minutes and enter. Act as if nothing has happened and ask for your money again. Do not be afraid; I will be there and the cadi will not dare harm you."

The next day, the lady gathered together her jewelry and took her daughter to the house of the cadi. She told her daughter, "When you see the chöpdji enter, wait a few minutes; then come and say, 'Father has just arrived from Egypt and is awaiting your return.'"

As planned, the lady then went to the cadi, carrying a box of precious jewels. She said, "Oh honorable cadi, my husband has asked me to join him in Egypt. I am afraid to take my jewelry on this long and dangerous journey. Will you keep them until my return? And in case I don't return, you may keep them as a token of my esteem."

She opened the bag and spilled the jewels into the cadi's open palms. Just at that moment, the chöpdji entered and said, "Oh wise one, your servant has come for the savings you have been guarding."

Because the cadi wanted to impress the wealthy woman and gain control of her jewels, he said, "Of course, I will return your money." And then to the woman he said, "See how the people trust me. I have held this man's money; I will do the same for your jewels."

The cadi ordered his treasurer to give the chöpdji the five hundred piasters. As soon as the poor man was out the door with his money, the woman's daughter came rushing in. "Mother!" she cried. "Father has returned from Egypt and awaits your return."

The lady scooped the jewels from the cadi's hands and rushed out the door. "May you have a thousand years' happiness," she called as she left.

The cadi was thunderstruck. He sat in the empty room without the five hundred piasters or the handfuls of jewels. At last he stroked his beard and said, "For forty years, I have been a judge, and for forty years, never have I met a woman who was more clever than I."

Belva Ann Lockwood

1830–1917

In 1870, Belva Lockwood and fourteen other women entered law school at National University Law School (later George Washington University). Lockwood was a forty-year-old wife, mother, and former high school principal. Out of the fifteen women, only she and one other woman completed the two-year program. The university refused to grant their diplomas because the male students objected to women graduates. Lockwood tried the alternative of taking a three-day oral exam. The examiners refused to release her score. Lockwood wrote a letter to President Ulysses S. Grant, ex-officio president of the school:

> Sir: You are, or you are not, President of the National University Law School. If you are President, I desire to say to you that I have passed through the curriculum of study in this school, and am entitled to, and demand, my diploma. If you are not its President, then I ask that you take your name from its papers, and not hold out to the world to be what you are not.
>
> Very Respectfully,
> Belva A. Lockwood[1]

Within twenty-six days, without explanation, her diploma arrived. She was admitted to the District of Columbia bar and set up a private practice.

Several years later, she was hired to handle a copyright infringement suit in the U.S. Court of Claims. Lockwood applied for admission to the federal court; the court rejected her application. Court of Claims Chief Justice Charles C. Nott said, "A woman is without legal capacity to take the office of attorney."[2] He suggested if Lockwood wished to practice in federal courts, she should write a law and get it passed.

Lockwood drafted a bill proposing that any woman who had practiced law for three years in any state should be allowed to practice before the U.S. Supreme Court. The legislation, which came to be known as "Mrs. Lockwood's Bill," had to be introduced three times before it passed. In 1879, Lockwood became the first woman lawyer admitted to the Supreme Court's bar.[3]

Lockwood also founded the first suffrage group in the District of Columbia and lobbied Congress for passage of feminist legislation. She ran for president in 1884 on the Equal Rights ticket and garnered 4,149 votes—all from men, since women were not allowed to vote.

As a lawyer, Lockwood defended thousands and won many historic cases. In her old age she again faced her adversary Charles C. Nott over money owed to the Cherokee Nation.

Historically, the Cherokee ancestral towns, farms, and hunting grounds were in the Great Smoky Mountains of North Carolina, Tennessee, Alabama, and Georgia. During the western expansion, white settlers wanted the rich, cleared Cherokee land and the gold discovered in Georgia. In 1830, the year Lockwood was born, the U.S. Congress passed the Indian Removal Bill, which would relocate all Indians to lands west of the Mississippi.

The Cherokees challenged the removal laws by establishing an independent Cherokee Nation. In 1832, the U.S. Supreme Court ruled in favor of the Cherokee. In *Worcester v. Georgia*, Justice John Marshall ruled that the Cherokee Nation was sovereign, the removal laws were invalid against this sovereign nation, and the Cherokee would have to voluntarily agree to removal in a treaty.

In the Treaty of New Echota, the U.S. government promised $1 million and Oklahoma land in exchange for the Cherokee lands. Only seventy-nine out of nearly seventeen thousand Cherokee signed the treaty, but President Jackson claimed it was a binding agreement.[4] In 1838, troops gathered fourteen thousand Cherokee and marched them to Oklahoma along the Trail of Tears. More than a thousand Cherokee escaped the deportation by hiding in the Great Smoky Mountains.

The government did not pay the million-dollar purchase price. Decades later, the Cherokee sued to recover the treaty money plus interest. The Eastern Cherokee, the descendants of those who had escaped, joined the suit. In 1891, Belva Lockwood was hired to represent fifteen thousand Eastern Cherokee. During fourteen years of preparation, she reviewed treaties and statutes, collected thousands of sworn statements from descendants, tried seventeen associated land cases, and filed briefs and petitions for her clients.

In 1905, the case was heard in the Court of Claims before Judge Charles Nott, the same judge who had denied Lockwood's admission to that court. Although acknowledging the government owed $1 million promised in the treaty, he refused to award all of the interest that the Cherokee sought. Lockwood appealed to the U.S. Supreme Court.

At the age of seventy-six, Lockwood made an impassioned plea before the Supreme Court for restitution for the Eastern Cherokee. The justices said she made "the most eloquent argument of any of the attorneys before the court."[5] Lockwood won the case and $5 million for her clients, $4 million of which was interest. On the day of the decree, Judge Nott met his old adversary on the courtroom steps; he shook Lockwood's hand and congratulated her on her success.

DOING
OUR PART

What I can do—I will
Though it be little as a daffodil.
          —Emily Dickinson

Holding up the Sky

China

Once, when Elephant was out walking, he saw something in the road. As he drew closer, he saw it was a hummingbird, lying on her back with her feet straight up in the air.

Elephant leaned over and whispered, "Are you dead?"

"No," she said.

"Are you hurt?" he asked.

"No," she said.

"Are you resting?"

"No."

"Then why are you lying in the middle of the road?"

"Because I heard the sky is going to fall. I am ready to hold it up."

Elephant taunted the bird, "Do you think those tiny feet can hold up the sky?"

"I don't know," the hummingbird said. "But we must do what we can do."

Justine Merritt
1924–

Why not tie a peace ribbon around the Pentagon? That was Justine Merritt's inspiration in 1982.

Merritt, a former teacher, was increasingly troubled about the threat of nuclear war. While at a Ignacian retreat, praying for guidance for her life, a line from the poem "The Gift" came to her mind: "I've prayed, do not let the world be destroyed."[1] At that moment Merritt heard a call to work for peace. At first she expected to follow the traditional course—ringing doorbells, signing petitions, and writing letters to politicians for a nuclear freeze. A month after the retreat, however, she decided instead to tie a ribbon around the Pentagon. She thought, "It will be just like tying a ribbon around your finger. It will serve as a gentle reminder that we love the earth and its people."[2]

Merritt had no money to finance the project. She initially sent a hundred letters to friends and family on her Christmas card list. As the project information passed informally from friend to friend and from family to family, the participants grew to include thousands in all fifty states and many foreign countries. The Ribbon became an official project of the Church Women United, an ecumenical religious organization. Participation came from such diverse sources as a convent in Indiana, a condominium in Florida, farms in Iowa, a quilting group in Montana, inmates in a California jail, and schoolchildren in the Netherlands.

From the beginning, Merritt's vision of the Ribbon was panels of fabric strung together, each one depicting the theme *What I cannot bear to think of as lost forever in nuclear war.* For her own panel Merritt spent seven hundred hours embroidering the names of family and loved ones who would be lost in a nuclear war. She said:

> When I was making my own Ribbon panel, I found that as I would thread my needle, I was confronting the fear, confronting the grief and terror. As I drew the needle up through the cloth, I was praying for peace, and the prayer became an affirmation of life. The very task of creating my panel helped empower me to face the reality of living in a nuclear age.[3]

The Peace Ribbon's panels measured thirty-six inches by eighteen inches. Ribbons were sewn to the corners of each panel so they could be tied in one long banner. More than twenty-five thousand panels were embroidered, silk-screened, tie-dyed, quilted, or appliquéd. Some panels were made with mementos of family life—wedding handkerchiefs, christening dresses, teddy bears, diapers. The motifs included home, family, pets, flowers, Earth, Bible verses, handprints, rainbows. One panel had a giant cockroach with rhinestone eyes imposed above the question, *Will they be the only survivors?*[4]

On August 4, 1985, over twenty thousand people tied a fifteen-mile peace ribbon around the Pentagon, the Capitol, and the Lincoln and Washington memorials. The date commemorated the fortieth anniversaries of the atomic bombings of Hiroshima and Nagasaki. The gathering was not intended to be a hostile demonstration but rather "quiet, prayerful, and contemplative."[5] There were no speeches or protests, just participants holding the Ribbon and meeting the spectators viewing the panels. While the ceremony was underway, President Reagan left the White House for Camp David. Neither Reagan nor any official representative acknowledged the Ribbon. Board member Mary Jo Peterson said, "Reagan sort of blew off the whole thing. We could see him flying over us at the end of the day..."[6]

After the event, panels were given to state coordinators and museums, such as the Peace Museum of Chicago. The Ribbon panels continued to be used at demonstrations. In 1986, panels were taken to a peace vigil at a Nevada nuclear test site.[7] Photographs of 350 panels are depicted in the book, *The Ribbon: A Celebration of Life*.

Many participants said that while they were uncertain about any direct results on government policy or public attitudes, their work and participation had been personally significant. Mary Frances Jaster, national coordinator for the Ribbon, said that the process of making her panel was a way of confronting her despair and reaffirming her ability to take action in what otherwise seemed a hopeless situation.[8] Merritt said, "All over this nation, people have threaded their fears into prayers for peace, creating something beautiful to affirm the hope present in all our lives."[9]

FOLLOWING OUR MEN INTO WAR

And Ruth said, Entreat me not to leave thee,
or to return from following after thee:
for whither thou goest, I will go;
and where thou lodgest, I will lodge…
    —Ruth 1:16

The Cruel War is Raging

American Civil War Folksong

The cruel war is raging and Johnny has to fight,
I want to be with him from morning till night.
I want to be with him, it grieves my heart so,
Oh, let me go with you; no, my love, no.

I'd go to your captain, get down upon my knees,
Ten thousand gold guineas I would give for your release;
Ten thousand gold guineas, it grieves my heart so,
Won't you let me go with you?—no, my love, no.

Tomorrow is Sunday and Monday is the day
Your captain calls for you and you must obey;
Your captain calls for you, it grieves my heart so,
Won't you let me go with you?—no, my love, no.

Your waist is too slender, your fingers are too small,
Your cheeks are too rosy to face the cannonball;
Your cheeks are too rosy, it grieves my heart so,
Won't you let me go with you?—no, my love, no.

Johnny, oh Johnny, I think you are unkind,
I love you far better than all other mankind;

I love you far better than tongue can express,
Won't you let me go with you?—yes, my love, yes.

I'll roach back my hair, men's clothing I'll put on,
I'll pass for your comrade as we march along;
I'll pass for your comrade and none can ever guess,
Won't you let me go with you?—yes, my love, yes.

Margaret Cochran Corbin
1751–1800

Margaret Cochran Corbin is an honored hero of the Revolutionary War. At twenty-one, Margaret married John Corbin. Four years later, when John joined the Continental Army, Margaret went with him. Wives of the soldiers often followed the troops, cooked for the men, washed their laundry, and nursed wounded soldiers.[1]

On November 16, 1776, while John was stationed at Fort Washington, New York, the fort was attacked by British Redcoats and Hessian mercenaries. When the gunner John was assisting was killed, he took charge of the cannon with Margaret's assistance. When John was killed, Margaret continued loading and firing the cannon until she was wounded by three grapeshot. Soldiers carried her to the rear, where she received first aid. The British captured the fort and paroled the wounded American soldiers, who were ferried across the river to Fort Lee. Margaret was then taken all the way to Philadelphia in a jolting wagon.

"Captain Molly," as she came to be known, continued to be included on regimental muster lists until the end of the war in 1783. She never fully recovered and was without the use of her left arm for the rest of her life. In 1779, the Continental Congress granted her a pension:

> Resolved,—That Margaret Corbin, wounded and disabled at the battle of Fort Washington, while she heroically filled the post of her husband, who was killed by her side serving a piece of artillery, do receive during her natural life, or continuance of said disability, one-half the monthly pay drawn by a soldier in service of these States and she now receive out of public stores, one suit of clothes or value thereof in money.[2]

Margaret Cochran Corbin died near West Point, New York, prior to her fiftieth birthday. She is honored with two memorials—one at West Point and the other in Manhattan. In 1926, the Daughters of the American Revolution had her remains moved from an obscure grave and reinterred with other soldiers behind the Old Cadet Chapel at West Point. A monument bears a bas-relief depicting the brave woman firing her husband's cannon. In Manhattan, near the site of the battle in Fort Tryon Park, a bronze plaque commemorates Margaret Cochran Corbin as "the first American woman to take a soldier's part in the War for Liberty."[3]

PRESERVING OUR WISDOM

Cast me not off in the time of old age;
forsake me not when my strength faileth.
—Psalm 71:9

The Wise Old Woman

Rumania

Once, when times were hard, a cruel young king commanded that all the old people should be taken into the forest and abandoned. "We don't have enough food for their useless mouths," he said. "They have lived their lives; now let us live ours."

The younger people did not like the command, but they did nothing when the soldiers came and marched away with their parents, grandparents, and everyone over fifty.

Only one son refused to send his mother away. He hid the old woman in the cellar and shared what little food he had with her. After all, she had given him life and sustained it. He would not abandon her.

The hard times continued and a drought withered the crops in the fields. At harvest time, there was little grain for bread. There was even less feed for the cattle and sheep. The winter came and the winds blew through empty barns. Everyone worried that spring would come and there would be no seeds for crops. The famine would continue.

During the cold, dark months, the son went into the cellar to share his scanty food with his mother and talk about the old days of plenty. When he at last asked her advice about the famine, she replied, "Don't tell anyone about this yet, but when the snow melts, take your plow and dig up the lane in front of our house.

Rake over it and stop worrying."

The son followed his mother's advice. When the snow melted and the lane was soft with warm mud, he plowed, raked, and waited. After the first spring rain, small spouts began to grow in the lane—wheat, oats, barley, even beans.

Word spread about the miracle. How could a man reap what he had not sown? Even the king came to see the growing crops.

He asked the young farmer, "What did you do? How did you know how to do it?"

The son tried to answer the king's questions, but he was confused and uncertain. Finally, he said, "I followed my mother's advice."

"Your mother?" said the king. "She is long gone to the forest."

"No, she is here, alive and well." The son brought his mother out of the cellar and into the sun.

"How did you get crops to grow in the roadway?" asked the king.

She replied, "I have lived many years and learned many things. When I was a child, we had a famine and my father plowed the lane and crops grew." She continued, "Your Majesty, think of all the carts that have driven over this road taking crops to market. Think of all the seeds that fell on the road from wheat, oats, barley, even beans. I did what my father taught me."

Upon hearing the old woman's wisdom, the king issued three orders. "First, everyone must go to the forest to find our elders. Second, everyone must plow, rake, and water the lanes in front of his house. Third, everyone must come to a great feast."

And so the king's orders were obeyed. The old people came back to their families. The crops grew and were harvested. A banquet was held. "I was wrong to think the old were useless," the king admitted. "We need their wisdom."

From that day on, the old and young prospered together. And the wise old woman was treated with much honor.

Maggie Kuhn

1905–1995

In 1970, Maggie Kuhn was forced to retire on her sixty-fifth birthday from her job of twenty-five years with the United

Presbyterian Church. "What I was going to do in my old age was not clear but I knew that I didn't want to just vegetate, and I knew I would if I stayed at home."[1]

Kuhn met with six acquaintances who also were facing retirement and were interested in social change. They sent messages to all the retired people they knew to form a coalition for social justice. They first called themselves Consultation of Older and Younger Adults for Social Change. But they became the Gray Panthers after the name was suggested by a television producer. In 1973, the Gray Panthers merged with Ralph Nader's Retired Professional Action Group.

The members did not want to get mired in what Kuhn called "old folks' issues" but to focus instead on matters that affected people of all ages. The organization's credo stated that it would advocate for "fundamental social change that will eliminate injustice, discrimination and oppression in our present society."[2] Kuhn said, "Young and old can and should work together for social change. Their needs and concerns are not mutually exclusive."[3]

One of their initial priorities was protesting the war in Vietnam. Soon the activists were staging sit-ins and picket lines to champion a variety of causes: government-subsidized health insurance, a ban on mandatory retirement, and a ban on nuclear weapons. "Out of the rocking chair, into the street!" was one of Kuhn's battle cries.[4]

Kuhn, a diminutive woman made shorter by osteoporosis, wore her gray hair pinned up in a bun and half-glasses pushed down on her nose. She took pride in looking her age. Once, while at the White House to watch Gerald Ford sign a pension bill, Kuhn repeatedly raised her hand to make a comment on the legislation. The President finally noticed her: "And what have you to say, young lady?" Kuhn, not to be patronized, replied, "Mr. President, I am not a young lady. I'm an old woman."[5]

She was listed in the *World Almanac* as one of the twenty-five most influential women in America. Until 1983, Kuhn traveled 150,000 miles each year lobbying and giving talks. She wrote four books: *You Can't Be Human Alone, Maggie Kuhn on Aging, Let's Get Out There and Do Something About Injustice,* and her autobiography, *No Stone Unturned.*

About her own death, Kuhn predicted, "I think I'll die in 1995. I think I can make it to ninety. I'd like to die in an airport on my way to a meeting."[6] She was right about the time of her death. Although she died at her home in Philadelphia instead of on a trip, she had picketed with striking transit workers only two weeks prior.

At her memorial service, Dieter Hessel, Director of the Ecumenical Program on Ecology, Justice, and Faith in Princeton, New Jersey, called her a "true elder of the tribe" and a "major figure in American social history." He observed, "Maggie Kuhn died on Earth Day and her memorial service is on Arbor Day. How appropriate for someone who cared deeply about the whole creation, especially flowers and cats, even as she worked for justice and peace among humans."[7]

Not Roses

In youth, we are like a flower
blooming in the greenhouse.
We don't know the world.
We haven't experienced pain yet
We haven't felt the wind, the rain,
the snows burying us in winter,
the miraculous rebirth of spring.
In age, we turn into wildflowers.
—Ai Ja Lee[1]

If women are not roses, what kind of flowers are they?

All the splendid varieties of wildflowers that Mother Nature seeded across the earth. Aren't women sunflowers, bold and tall? Or butter-and-eggs, common and showy? Or night-blooming cereus, the "queen-of-the-night," ephemeral and exotic?

The stories in this section are about women as unrestrained as wildflowers. They dwell in prairies, deserts, and bogs. Perhaps they took root in a cottage garden but escaped on the wind. Generally they flourish where they will, with care from no man's hand. For example, the first woman, Lilith, refuses to be dominated by Adam and flies away from Eden on wings of fire.

These women are not the norm: they are gamblers, witches, defiant wives. Wildflower women suit themselves and follow their inner urgings. They may savor notoriety, food, or sex. They may pursue revenge, demand restitution, or agitate for their rights. They may do good for others, but often their unconventional methods challenge the establishment. For example, Sarah Bagley seeks a ten-hour work day for mill workers, so she organizes one of the first strikes against mill owners.

Writer Carolyn Heilbrun says women need a hero myth that inspires them "to take risks, to make noise, to be courageous, to become unpopular."[2] These audacious, authentic, and highly competent women provide models for living nontraditional lives in traditional cultures. They are peers for women who were born and remain wildflowers. They are mentors for women who surrendered their exuberance in early adolescence. They are examples for women who, in age, seek to become wildflowers.

BREAKING FREE
OF CONVENTION

Women's fall from grace came not with the eating of forbidden fruit but through suppression.
—Lynn Gottlieb, *She Who Dwells Within*

Lilith

Israel

Some say on the Sixth Day, God created Adam from dust collected from all parts of the earth. God created Adam perfect and balanced, neither male or female, but both at once. In due time, the female part separated and became Lilith. She was comely with long hair and a necklace of fragrant lilies around her throat. She had wings of fire.

Adam and Lilith never found peace together but bickered over matters large and small. Adam wished to rule over Lilith. When he wanted to lie with her, he commanded her to lie in the recumbent position.

"Why must I lie beneath you?" she asked.

"I am your lord and master, and it is your duty to obey me."

"I was created with you from dust and therefore am your equal," said Lilith. "I will not submit to you."

In a rage, she uttered the Ineffable Name of God, spread her wings, and flew away. Some say when Lilith left the garden, she flew to a cave by the Red Sea, took demons for lovers, and gave birth to multitudes of demons.

Adam called to his Creator, "Sovereign of the universe! The woman has run away."

God sent three angels, Senoy, Sansenoy, and Semangeloph, to bring her back. Lilith told them, "I refuse to return to Eden."

The angels said, "We will slay one hundred of your demon children each day until you return."

"Even this fate is better than submission to Adam." She vowed to visit men sleeping alone, steal their semen, and give birth to demon children to replace those slain every day.

When the angels slew one hundred of her children, Lilith proclaimed, "In return for my pain, I will slay the children of Adam." She swore to cause sickness to infants, and even their mothers, during childbirth. "If the infant is male, I shall have dominion over him for eight days after his birth, and if female, for twenty days."

Angry with her defiance, the angels tried to drown her. Lilith pacified them with a bargain: "If I enter a home and see your names on an amulet, I will have no power over that infant."

The angels let her go. And ever since, when Lilith sees all three angel's names—Senoy, Sansenoy, and Semangeloph—on the amulet of a young child, she remembers her oath, and does not harm the child.

When Lilith did not return to Eden, God said, "It is not good that the man should be alone." He put Adam in a deep sleep, took one of his ribs, and fashioned a helpmate for Adam. This woman became the mother of all people; she was called Eve.

Mae West

1893–1980

Mae West—sex icon, actor, author, playwright, producer, singer, dancer, and comic—was independent and unconventional. Her open sexuality brought her vilification and censorship on the stage, in the movies, and on the radio.

West was born in Brooklyn August 17, 1893, to an ex-boxer and a corset model. At eight years of age, she sang and danced in amateur vaudeville productions. By 1909, West was working in the theater and touring the country. An older colleague, alarmed at West's reckless behavior with men, advised her to get married and "play it safe."

At seventeen, she hastily married Frank Wallace, her nineteen-year-old musical partner. She was not in love with him and regretted her marriage immediately. "It's just this physical thing," she told him. "You don't move my finer instincts." Wallace promised to keep their marriage secret and stayed out of sight for over twenty-five years.[1]

She never married again. In later years, West said, "I knew I couldn't have both marriage and a career...If I hadn't made such a big success, I'd regret it. If I hadn't got to the top, I'd be sorry. But as it is you can't do two things in life."

In 1925, West was thirty-two years old and still a mediocre vaudevillian. Then she wrote and starred in a play, simply titled *SEX*. West played a prostitute on a quest for adventure. The navy was in port and the sailors came to the play in droves. West lent every imaginable nuance and innuendo to her lines.

After forty-one weeks, the police raided the play and arrested the cast, producers, and directors on corruption charges. West fought the charges against her, recalling later, "I enjoyed the courtroom as just another stage." When she played to the packed courtroom, the judge asked, "Miss West, are you trying to show contempt for this court?" She answered, "On the contrary, Your Honor, I was doin' my best to conceal it."

West said the prosecutor could not find "one line or one word in the play that was profane, lewd, lascivious, or obscene." Instead, he claimed "Miss West's personality, looks, walk, mannerisms, and gestures made the lines and situations suggestive."

The testimony focused on her belly dance performed to "St. Louis Blues," in which West danced fully clothed in a tight metallic gown. One of the arresting officers testified, "Miss West moved her navel up and down and from right to left."

West's lawyer questioned, "Did you actually see her navel?"

"No," replied the officer. "But I saw something in her middle move from east to west." The courtroom erupted in laughter.[2]

The verdict: guilty of corrupting the morals of youth. The sentence: ten days in jail. After serving eight days at Welfare Island, she was released for "good behavior."

In 1928, West gave herself the lead role in her play *Diamond Lil*. The show, set in the Bowery during the gay 1890s, was a hit. As Diamond Lil, West became the almost-respectable toast of Broadway. She also had found the persona she would adopt for the rest of her life.

At the age of thirty-nine, she began her movie career with

Paramount. Her first role was a bit part supporting George Raft in *Night After Night*. Unhappy with the role, she rewrote her dialogue. In one short scene, West sauntered into a nightclub, hand on hip, and draped in diamonds. The hat-check attendant remarked, "Goodness, what beautiful diamonds." West responded, "Goodness had nothing to do with it, dearie." The scene catapulted her into motion picture history. Raft said, "She stole everything but the cameras."

Her first starring role was in *She Done Him Wrong*, the film version of her play *Diamond Lil*. The film broke box-office records and saved the nearly bankrupt Paramount company from selling out to MGM. Over the next two years, her films earned over a million dollars' profit. West became the most highly paid and sought-after female star in America. Depression American loved the risqué and bejeweled blonde.

Like her art, West's personal life did not conform to social standards. Her affairs were many and included one with her leading man in *I'm No Angel*, Cary Grant. She was shunned in Hollywood.

West's notoriety brought her under the close scrutiny of the powerful Motion Picture Producers and Distributors of America, popularly known as "The Hays Office." Will Hays brought in a new censorship code in 1934 to combat West's perceived threat to American morality. One week before the premiere of *She Done Him Wrong*, for example, the Hays Office forced Paramount to recall the prints. The censors were shocked at West's rendition of the song "A Guy What Takes His Time" (or "Slow Motion Man"). West's languid delivery made the mild lyrics seem like a graphic tribute to slow lovemaking. All but the first and last verses had to be deleted before release.[3]

NBC Radio banned West after an "Adam and Eve" skit on the *Chase and Sanborn Hour,* starring Edgar Bergen and Charlie McCarthy. Eve (West) describes Adam (Don Ameche) as "long, lazy and lukewarm." The bored Eve wants to leave the Garden, but Adam says they cannot go unless he eats an apple from the forbidden tree. Eve tempts the serpent (Charlie McCarthy) into picking an apple for her. "Now get me a big one," she says. "I feel like doing a big apple." Adam eats the apple and God throws them out of Eden.[4]

Congressmen and clergymen alike attacked the broadcast as obscene. Although the show attracted the biggest audience ever, the general manager of NBC banned her or any mention of her name on the network. West commented about the furor:

> There was nothing offensive in the dialogue or it would have never got on the air in the first place. I only gave the lines my characteristic delivery. What else could I do? I wasn't Aimee Semple McPherson. Or Lincoln at Gettysburg, or John Foster Dulles, or even Eleanor Roosevelt. I was Mae West. Sunday on radio doesn't alter one's personality.[5]

The constant editing and censorship diluted her racy style of comedy. After nine movies, West decided to abandon films. *The Heat's On* for Columbia Pictures in 1943 was her final movie until *Myra Breckinridge* in 1974.

She worked occasionally on the stage and the nightclub circuit. When she was sixty, she played a successful tour of Vegas. She sang "I Like to Do All Day What I Do All Night" surrounded by a chorus of "muscle men." In 1957 she wrote her autobiography, *Goodness Had Nothing To Do With It.*

As she aged, West gradually became replaced by female impersonators who looked more like her than she did. Fortunately, West had invested wisely in Hollywood real estate. She lived in Los Angeles, in her Art Deco apartment decorated with mirrors and statues of herself, until, at the age of eighty-seven, she died of a stroke.

FIGHTING
FOR FREEDOM

Out of the ash
I rise with my red hair
and I eat men like air.
  —Sylvia Plath, "Lady Lazarus"

Boadicea: Warrior Queen

Ancient Britain

In London, near the River Thames, there is a bronze statue of Boadicea (also spelled *Boudicca*) driving a chariot pulled by two rearing horses. The monument honors the Celtic warrior queen who fought the Romans almost two thousand years ago. Her rebellion was chronicled by the Roman historian Tacitus in approximately 100 A.D. Tacitus heard the story from his father-in-law, Agricola, who was in Britain at the time of Boadicea's battles.[1]

For a hundred years, the Romans had ruled Britain loosely. But the rule turned harsh under an ambitious new Roman leader, Seutonius Paulinus; many tribes submitted to crippling taxes and property seizures.

Queen Boadicea ruled Iceni with her husband, Prasutagus. Their people were proud and prosperous farmers on the southern coast of England. Following the Roman invasion of Britain under Claudius in 43 A.D., King Prasutagus became a rich client-king of the Romans. King Prasutagus had no son, so to insure safety for his family after his death, he willed half his kingdom to the Roman Emperor Nero and half to his daughters, with Boadicea as regent. When the king died in 60 A.D., Tacitus described that what happened was the opposite of Prasutagus's intention:

> His dominions were ravaged by the centurions; the slaves pillaged his house, and his effects were seized as lawful plunder.

His wife, Boudicca, was disgraced with cruel stripes; her daughters were ravished, and the most illustrious of the Icenians were, by force, deprived of the positions which had been transmitted to them by their ancestors. The whole country was considered as a legacy bequeathed to the plunderers.[2]

Secretly, Boadicea recruited neighboring tribes for an uprising. Because the invading Roman forces were from Camulodunum (Colchester), the capital of Roman Britain, Boadicea's first objective was to capture Camulodunum. The colony and its temple—built by taxation to honor Claudius, the former emperor—were a source of hatred for the Britons.

While the revolt was being readied, strange events were reported:

While the Britons were preparing to throw off the yoke, the statue of victory, erected at Camulodunum, fell from its base, without any apparent cause, and lay extended on the ground with its face averted, as if the goddess yielded to the enemies of Rome. Women in restless ecstasy rushed among the people, and with frantic screams denounced impending ruin. In the council-chamber of the Romans hideous clamours were heard in a foreign accent; savage howlings filled the theatre, and near the mouth of the Thames the image of a colony in ruins was seen in the transparent water; the sea was purpled with blood, and, at the tide of ebb, the figures of human bodies were traced in the sand.[3]

The bulk of the Roman force, under the military governor, Seutonius, was away fighting Druids on the isle of Mona in north Wales. The time was right for revolt.

On the eve of battle, Boadicea addressed the troops. Her eyes burned with fury, her voice was harsh, and she brandished a spear as she commanded the army to attack Camulodunum. She was tall and strong, and her red hair hung to her knees. She wore a great twisted golden necklace and a tunic of many colors, over which lay a thick mantle fastened by a brooch.[4]

Suddenly she released a hare from the folds of her dress, "as a species of divination." The hare ran in "an auspicious direction" and the crowds cheered at the favorable omen. She prayed to Andraste, the Celtic war goddess for victory: "I thank thee, Andraste, and call upon thee as woman speaking to woman."[5]

Unguarded and unprepared, the town was surprised by the

assault. The handful of Roman soldiers retreated to the temple. After a two-day siege, the temple was destroyed and "the colony was laid waste with fire and sword."[6]

After her victory, Boadicea made a fatal mistake; before marching the sixty-three miles to London (Londinium), she allowed her undisciplined troops to waste two weeks celebrating and plundering. During that time, Roman troops left Wales and other outposts and rushed to unite against the rebel troops.

Seutonius reached London with a small cavalry attachment. He decided the prosperous trading center was indefensible and abandoned it to the enemy. Boadicea's force burst on London and slaughtered several thousand people, including the old, sick, and helpless. The mutilations and sufferings were chronicled by historians. Tacitus commented, "The halter and the gibbet, slaughter and defoliation, fire and sword, were the marks of savage valor. Aware that vengeance would overtake them, they were resolved to make sure of their revenge, and glut themselves with the blood of their enemies."[7]

With ranks growing to a hundred thousand, the British force marched to Verulamiun (St. Albans) and sacked the partially evacuated town. The Britons, who did not want prisoners or slaves, killed more than seventy-thousand Romans and allies in these three assaults.

Ten thousand seasoned Roman troops gathered to confront the rebels. Seutonius chose the site in the West Highlands: narrow at the entrance, encircled by woods, and sheltered by trees from rear ambush. The Roman governor placed his legions, six deep, in close formation in the center with the cavalry in the wings. The Britons, mostly farmers, bounded onto the plain in disorder. Their wives and families waited in wagons in the rear to observe another British victory.

The half-naked Britons rushed forward in homemade chariots and shot their spears and slings randomly. Boadicea drove through the ranks in a chariot with her two daughters urging on her troops. The Roman legionnaires held their ground; the front line discharged their javelins. The leaders of the British charge were struck down. Then the well-trained and well-armed Romans rushed forward in a wedge; the cavalry closed in.[8]

The overpowered Britons tried to retreat, but their wagons in the rear impeded their flight. "A dreadful slaughter followed. Neither sex nor age was spared. The cattle, falling in one promiscuous carnage, added to the heaps of the slain."[9] The Romans, losing only four hundred, killed as many as eighty thousand Britons. Boadicea took poison and died. The rebellion was over.

Lozen: Apache Warrior
ca. 1840–ca. 1890

Lozen was an Apache warrior, seer, and medicine woman. Her brother Victorio, leader of the Mimbres, or Warm Springs Apache, called her "my right hand." He said, "Strong as a man, braver than most, and cunning in strategy, Lozen is a shield to her people."[1]

Before the "opening of the West," the Apache people were distinct and autonomous bands roaming in New Mexico and Arizona.

Extended families lived in camps in wickiups, domes made of poles and covered with skins. The women gathered nuts and berries and grew vegetables; the men hunted game. The Apache also raided neighboring Indian groups and Mexicans, stealing horses, cattle, and booty.

In 1848, after winning the Mexican War, the United States government took possession of Arizona and New Mexico. Settlers moved into Indian Territory; gold miners flocked in the Mimbres' territory in New Mexico. The Butterfield Overland, a transcontinental stage line, cut through Cochise and Geronimo's territory near the Chiricahua Mountains in Arizona. Hostilities broke out and atrocities occurred on all sides. In response, the U.S. Army built forts and tried to subdue or exterminate the Indians.

During the administration of Ulysses S. Grant, Congress raised money to establish reservations. General George Crook ordered the Apache to "come to the reservation or die."[2] At first, the bands were put on reservations near their homelands. Then the government decided control would be easier if all Apache were relocated to one reservation. Five thousand Apache were forced into San Carlos, even though many bands were antagonists.

In May 1877, 453 Mimbres men, women, and children were forced to walk 250 miles from the reservation in New Mexico to the hot, treeless San Carlos Reservation in Arizona's barren eastern desert—or as some called it, "Hell's Forty Acres." A visitor to the reservation described the conditions:

> Take stone and ashes and thorns, with some scorpions and rattlesnakes thrown in, dump the outfit on stones, heat the

stones red hot, set the United States Army after the Apaches, and you have San Carlos.[3]

In August 1877, three hundred Apache fled from the San Carlos Reservation. They fled from hunger, smallpox, and temperatures of 140 degrees. On stolen horses, they crossed the Gila River to freedom. The bands of Apache divided and went their separate ways. One of the leaders was Victorio. His sister, Lozen, helped the women and children cross the river and then went to Victorio's side.

Lozen was about forty years of age at the time of the escape. She dressed like a man and fought like a man. She took part in warriors' ceremonies, sang war songs, and sat in council. The translation of her Apache name meant "dexterous horse thief." Lozen earned her name with feats like the one at the battle of Cibecue, where she rode into the Army camp and drove off the cavalry horses.

Riding with the warriors was unusual but possible, because Lozen was unmarried. Folk legend says that she remained unmarried because she loved a mysterious warrior called the Gray Ghost. When Lozen was sixteen, a handsome visitor had ridden into the Warm Springs camp on a magnificent stallion. He said he was a chief from another land. After he left, Lozen could not forget him and would accept no other man.[4]

Her greatest skill was the ability to find the enemy. While participating in her puberty ceremony, she kept a solitary four-day vigil at a sacred mountain. She received spiritual power to locate Apache foes. Before battle, she would stand with her arms outstretched and her open palms heavenward; she would sing to Ussen, the Creator:

Upon this earth
On which we live
Ussen has Power.
This Power is mine
For locating the Enemy.
I search for the Enemy
Which only Ussen the Great
Can show me.[5]

She would turn clockwise until she felt a tingling in her hands; the more intense the tingling, the closer the enemy. Her palms turned purple when they pointed toward the foe.

Lozen was also a gifted medicine woman. It was her duties as a medicine woman that separated her from Victorio when he needed her most. After the escape from San Carlos Reservation, the Mimbres Apache hid for months south of Texas, in the mountains of Mexico. Attempting to go home to Ojo Caliente, they crossed the Rio Grande, were ambushed by the cavalry, and galloped back to Mexico. Lozen stayed behind to care for a Mescalero Apache woman in labor.

For weeks after delivering the baby, Lozen protected the mother and child as she took them back to their people. She killed cattle for food, stole horses for transportation, and killed a cavalryman for his rifle. When she arrived at the Mescalero reservation, she learned the fate of her brother.

Victorio and the Mimbres had been pursued by U.S. troops and driven deep into the Mexican state of Chihuahua. On October 15, 1880, they were cornered by Mexican soldiers. Victorio and 175 men, women, and children were killed; 78 were captured; 30 escaped. Would such a tragedy have been prevented if Lozen had been there to warn of the enemy?[6]

Lozen rode out alone to search for the survivors. She tracked them down, and together they joined with Geronimo and the Chiricahua Apache. During the following years, Geronimo and his followers returned to and fled from the reservation many times. After Geronimo's final breakout in 1886, five thousand troops gave chase. The army crisscrossed the desert, guarded every water hole, and set up a network of flashing mirrors to send Morse code from the mountaintops.[7]

When Geronimo's followers were too exhausted to continue their flight, he sent Lozen to arrange meetings with the military. In 1886, the last free Apache surrendered: thirty-eight people, fourteen of them women and children.[8] Lozen is in several famous photos with the captured Geronimo and his warriors, dressed like a man. There is nothing to indicate that she is a woman.

Along with the other prisoners, Lozen was transported by train to the stone prison in Fort Pickens, a desolate island off the coast of Florida. Later, she was transferred to Mount Vernon Barracks in Alabama. She died there, presumably of tuberculosis, at the approximate age of fifty. Because the government did not list Indian prisoners by name, only by number, her death was not recorded. Her people buried her anonymously according to custom.

WELCOMING WIDOWHOOD

*In losing a husband one loses a master
who is often an obstacle to the enjoyment
of many things.*
—Madeleine de Scudery,
Clelia, An Excellent New Romance

The Really Dangerous Post

United States

Some good women end up with real dogs for husbands and decide that the only thing to do is to be patient. So it was for a certain farmer's wife. She kept a clean house, made a little egg money from her prize chickens, and baked fresh biscuits every morning. And what did she get for her patience? A lazy husband who would rather play poker and drink hard cider than tend his fields.

The years went by with her being patient and him being him, until one night a neighbor found him dead in a ditch. At first, everyone thought the farmer was just drunk. But the doctor declared him dead from a bad heart.

The widow dressed all in black and rode in the wagon that took the coffin to the cemetery. Six strong men heaved the coffin out of the wagon and carried it up the hill. One of the bearers stumbled and the coffin bumped against the gatepost. The jolt must have jarred the farmer back to life because he started groaning and hollering. When they pulled the lid off, the hung-over and recently deceased farmer sat up. He was carried back home instead of to his grave.

His brief visit to the ever-after did not cause him to mend his ways. So she kept on being patient, and he kept on being him. In about ten years, the farmer who was not dead really was. It seemed to be for good this time. But when the wagon went up to the cemetery, the widow hopped out, ran ahead of the bearers, stood against the gatepost and said, "Now, all of you, be careful. Watch out for this really dangerous post!"

Gertrude Franklin Horn Atherton
1857–1949

Gertrude Atherton was a merry widow, international flirt, and prolific writer. Atherton was born into San Francisco society, reared in private schools, and spoiled by her grandparents. At eighteen, the svelte, blond, and bored beauty eloped with her twice-divorced mother's latest boyfriend—the very Catholic, seemingly wealthy George Atherton. Her mother collapsed into a semi-coma and her grandfather disowned her.

The newlyweds moved to the Atherton ranch. Dominga Atherton, her 200-pound Spanish mother-in-law, tried to control the high-spirited bride and convert her to Catholicism. George failed at a brokerage business and at managing the family ranch. When the bridegroom could not and would not find a job, he moped around the house and spent the allowance from his family on himself.

In time, Gertrude Atherton produced two children and handed them over to her mother-in-law to raise; she preferred puppies to babies.[1] She turned to writing for money and solace from her stifling marriage. First, she earned $5 for brief articles for the San Francisco weekly, *The Argonaut*. Next, under a pseudonym, she earned $150 for a novel, *The Randolphs of Redwoods,* which ran in six installments in the *Argonaut*. The novel, which was a thinly disguised account of a local society woman turned alcoholic, shocked her husband and mother-in-law because of the passionate love scenes. "Ladies do not write," pronounced Dominga.[2] Gertrude was shunned by her aristocratic social circle for revealing society secrets.

The marital disharmony continued. Gertrude spent her $150 on books. George was angry because a "proper wife would have turned the money over to her husband to settle his debts."[3] Gertrude continued to write while George stalked in and out of her room, "pounding on the door if I locked it, and reviling the fates for inflicting him with a wife so different from the wives of others."[4]

She began to wish he was dead. Her writing was always self-revealing. One of her stories published in *Overland Monthly* featured a beautiful, intellectual woman married to the ne'er-do-well son of a wealthy family. The unhappy wife did not end her marriage but instead wrote and traveled alone.

Although Gertrude longed for travel, it was George who got the opportunity. George's Chilean cousin, who was an officer on the *Pilcomayo,* a naval man-of-war, invited him to sail from San Francisco to Chile. Gertrude was eager to be rid of him, and George left on his adventure.

Several months later, Gertrude's doorbell rang and a friend gave her the following newspaper report:

> The embalmed remains of George Atherton were brought to this city yesterday on board the barkentine *Tropic Bird*. It will be remembered that the deceased left this port about two months ago on the Chilean corvette *Pilcomayo* on a voyage for his health, and died on the passage to the Sandwich Islands. The deceased was well known in this city and had a very large circle of friends. The exact place of interment is not yet settled.[5]

George had developed a kidney stone at sea, hemorrhaged, and died. Instead of burying him at sea, the officers embalmed him in a barrel of rum. George was shipped back from Tahiti with a cargo of vanilla, oranges, and coconuts.

Upon hearing the news, Dominga tore off her clothes, took to bed, and screamed until exhausted. Gertrude never shed a tear.

George's body, which arrived with the heart cut out, was shelved in the family mausoleum. His heart was filed in a bank vault in Chile in a glass jar filled with alcohol.[6]

The delighted widow embarked on an international life in New York City, London, and Paris. She wrote a compulsory one thousand words each day before lunch and published almost a book a year until her death at ninety-one. Her perennial youth and beauty attracted many suitors, but she forswore marriage. Once she visited a French religious shrine to seek relief from writer's block. A French woman inquired if she had come to pray for a husband. Gertrude replied, "A husband! What is a husband compared to a book!"[7]

SEEKING REVENGE

"Don't get mad; get everything."
—Ivana Trump in the movie
The First Wives' Club

Perfect Justice

Urban Legend

A wife put an ad in the automobile section of the Sunday paper: CHERRY RED PORSCHE, 2,000 MI., MAKE ANY OFFER, (555) 555–2222.

Just after the dawn paper delivery, her phone rang. It was an eager college student. "How much?"

She replied, "Come out and see it; make any offer."

The student came out to take a look at the Porsche. It was even more beautiful than he'd imagined. "It has all the bells and whistles," he said in awe. "But I haven't enough money even to make an offer."

"How much money do you have in your checking account?" the wife inquired.

"About seventy-five dollars," he replied.

"That's just the offer I am looking for," said the wife. "Sold!"

"You have got to be kidding," said the student. "What's the catch? Is it broken? Is it stolen?"

"No, this is a perfectly legitimate deal. Write a check and then sign the title," she replied. They formalized the sale. Before the student drove away, he made one last inquiry, "Tell me the truth. Why did you sell this car for seventy-five dollars?"

"Well," the wife told him, "that's my husband's car. He bought it about the same time he joined the Hairpiece Club and hired a new secretary. Last week, he and she left on a plane for Hawaii.

Yesterday, he called and said he needed money. He asked me to sell his new Porsche and send the money to him. I'm mailing your check today."

Marilyn Nichols Kane
1948–

Marilyn Nichols Kane's ex-husband has been called "America's worst deadbeat dad." Jeffrey Nichols owed an estimated $640,000 in back child support. For five years, he moved from New York to Canada to Florida to Vermont to avoid paying. As a result, he was in trouble with a New York state court and the federal government.

Kane and Nichols met at New York University in 1968. After marriage and three children, Nichols became a precious-metals consultant and vice-president with Goldman Sachs, earning $160,000 a year. In 1985, Nichols told his wife, "I really just don't love you anyone."[1] He moved out but continued to support his family. Four years later, after beginning a new relationship, he disappeared. The money stopped coming. In April 1989, Nichols sent a postcard from Hawaii: *Marilyn, having a ball. Glad you're not here!*[2]

In August 1990, Kane obtained a divorce in New York on grounds of abandonment. New York Supreme Court Judge Phyllis Gangel-Jacobs ordered Nichols to pay $9,362.82 a month in child support. Kane located him in Toronto and got a Canadian court order instructing Nichols to pay. Nichols and his new wife left Canada to avoid payment.

Kane tracked him to Florida where he was president of his own company, American Precious Metals Advisor. Nichols told the Florida court that he would not pay child support because the children were not his. After a year of legal battles and DNA tests that proved he was the father, Nichols fled again.

Meanwhile, Nichols' finances had become public when, in August 1994, the second wife filed for divorce. She swore in an affidavit that Nichols had earned more than $400,000 in that year and hid money from Kane in a British West Indies bank account.[3] Although Kane had remarried and was financially secure, she was relentless in her pursuit, "I never, never, never thought about giving up."[4] She found Nichols in Vermont, living in a $500,000 house bought in his second wife's name.

The chase was over. In August 1995, Nichols was arrested by the Federal Bureau of Investigation on charges of fleeing from state to state to avoid paying child support. The Child Support Recovery Act of 1992 made it a federal crime to cross state lines to avoid paying child support. Later, Nichols pleaded guilty to the federal charges. He was sentenced to six months in jail, the maximum sentence, and ordered to repay $623,955. Federal judge Loretta Preska said that Nichols had "made a career since 1990 of flouting court orders."[5]

He was arrested again on a New York State warrant for contempt of court. Taken in handcuffs into the New York court to explain why he had not paid support for his children, he pleaded for compassion; his second wife had died from lung cancer, his business had collapsed, he had $5 left in his checking account.

Judge Gangel-Jacobs, who had presided over the divorce, ordered Nichols held until he paid $68,000 of the amount owed. Nichols spent four months in jail until he reached an agreement to pay Kane in installments.

When payments were not forthcoming, the judge ordered an auction of the contents of Nichols' large Vermont house to pay some of the money he owed. On August 18, 1996, over 350 people attended the auction and cheered when Kane was introduced. She later told the press that she cried when she saw the jewelry, antiques, and crystal. "I feel so appalled at what this man accumulated in five years when he was not supporting his children."[6] Kane called the auction "perfect justice."

GETTING THE JOB DONE

The rooster crows, but the hen delivers the goods.
—old Texas saying

The Old Woman and Her Maids

Greece

Once there was an old woman who worked her own farm. She was small, stringy, and full of zip. One morning, after the rooster crowed, she tied on her bonnet. "I'm going to hire some help," she said. She bustled into town and hired three hefty maids. Unfortunately, she did not know the maids liked feather pillows better than they liked feather dusters.

On the walk back, the little old woman stepped lively and lectured about life on the farm. "We get up early and get it done," she said. "Morning is the best time."

The maids dillydallied and whined and whispered behind her back, "Morning is the best time . . . to sleep!"

The little old woman told the first maid, "You'll milk the cows."

She told the second maid, "You'll slop the hogs."

She told the third, "You'll feed the chickens."

The maids walked even slower after they heard the news.

The next morning, when the rooster crowed, the three maids stumbled out to the barnyard. The rooster stepped lively across the fence, fixed them with a bright eye, ruffled his tailfeathers, and ordered:

Cock-a-doddle-do.
Get up and get it done.

119

Cock-a-doddle-do.
Get up and get it done.
Morning is the best time.

The maids sidled by the rooster and stuck out their tongues, but they got it all done. They milked the cows, slopped the hogs, and fed the chickens—even that bossy rooster.

And so it went, day after day on the farm—fetching and carrying and feeding the animals. But the absolutely worst thing was hearing that rooster in the early hours:

Cock-a-doddle-do.
Get up and get it done.
Cock-a-doddle-do.
Get up and get it done.
Morning is the best time.

At night, instead of sleeping, the maids muttered about what they wanted to do with to the rooster.

The first said, "I'd like to bop the Boss on the head."

The second said, "I'd like to bop him on the head and wring his neck."

The third said, "I'd like to bop him on the head and wring his neck and pull out his tailfeathers."

And the more they muttered about murdering the old rooster, the better it sounded. Silencing that barnyard bird would solve all their problems. They could sleep late. They could meander through the day without enduring his *"get up and get it done."*

Finally, they talked themselves into the deed. In the dark of the moon, the trio crept through the barnyard and grabbed that rooster off the fence before he could make a sound. They bopped him on the head; they wrung his neck; they pulled out his tailfeathers. They put him in a sack and threw him down the river. Then they went to bed for a good night's sleep.

The next morning *everyone* slept late. The sun was high in the sky before the old woman opened her eyes and let out a cry: "We're late!" She ran into the yard—the fence was empty. She searched for her dear rooster, but all she found was a tailfeather.

She woke the maids with the tragic news. She sat at the foot of their big feather bed, blew her nose, and said, "Girls, the Boss is gone. Who will get us up to get it done?"

When the maids walked by the fence where the old bird had preened, paraded, and posed, they stuck out their tongues at the empty air. Then they smiled at each other.

That night the trio got ready for bed in a leisurely fashion. They savored sleeping late, waking with the sun on their faces, and hearing the quiet of the country.

But the next morning, a hubbub jolted the maids out of their sleep: *"Cock-a-doodle-do! Get up and get it done."*

The little old woman strutted into their room—the tailfeather stuck in her bonnet. *"Cock-a-doodle-do! Get up and get it done."*

She said, "I must carry on for my dearly departed rooster. The Boss would have wanted it that way."

When the maids stumbled into the barnyard, half dressed and shaky, they saw it was not yet dawn.

"We're up a bit early today," said the little old woman. "Because my dearly departed rooster wasn't here, I worried about oversleeping. It's better to get a good start on the day, isn't it girls? Morning is the best time."

The next morning, the little old woman strutted down the hall and crowed at their door—a bit earlier than the morning before. And so it went, morning after morning, strutting and crowing, earlier and earlier. Soon the chores were done before the sun rose.

The maids began to reminisce for the days when the rooster let them sleep until morning light. They even offered to pay for a new rooster—from their own wages.

"Thank you for your kindness," the little old woman said, "but no one can replace the Boss."

Grandmother and the Rooster

One of the early pioneers in Washington State told her granddaughter Margaret Dykeman about the hardships of crossing the plains, being widowed, and being left with six boys to raise. She told about planting her first garden in Cowlitz County:

> I had a half cupful of seed corn; I had carried it with me across the plains. There was no more to be had. I dug up the ground and was dropping in each precious piece when I saw

my old rooster had sneaked up behind me. He was following along and gobbling the corn. I didn't hesitate; I killed that rooster, cut open his crop, took out the seed, and replanted it.[1]

OUTWITTING HOME INTRUDERS

If you mess with me, you've got a world of trouble.

—A. Elizabeth "Bessie" Delany, at age 100

The Old Woman and the Tengu

Japan

An old woman lived alone in a hut back in the forest and away from the village. With courage and wit, she managed to survive.

One dark, frosty night, she built a small fire from wood she had gathered that day. She heard a knock at her door. *No one has ever come here at night,* she thought.

"Who is it?" she asked in a soft voice.

The knock on the door grew louder.

"Who is there?" she said in a louder voice.

The knocking turned into banging. The old woman shouted over the din, "What do you want?"

When the door looked like it was going to splinter from the blows, she flung it open to face the intruder. There stood her worst nightmare—a tengu with a big nose and an angry face. The demon pushed her aside and walked to the fire. He began to rub his hands together and slap his wings to chase away the chill. "Make me some tea. And make it hot." The old woman hurried as best she could, and all the while she kept a brave face.

After the tengu drank several bowls of steaming tea, he did not look quite so angry. For the first time he turned and took a long look at the old woman. "I really scare you, don't I?"

"No, you don't scare me. A cold traveler is welcome in my humble hut." The old woman looked the tengu straight in the eye. "Do I scare you?"

The tengu burst into laughter. "An old woman scare me! How funny!"

Before the tengu had stopped laughing, the old woman asked, "Then what does scare you?"

And before the tengu could think, he replied, "Bushes and brush growing in thickets. My wings get tangled in thickets; I get caught. I hate thickets."

Then the demon asked the woman, "What are you most scared of?"

"Dongo."

"Granny, why are you afraid of sweet little cake balls?" the tengu asked.

"Because they are sticky and tasty and I eat so many that I am sick for days." She lowered her voice, "But I am really most scared of little gold coins."

"No! Not gold coins," the incredulous demon gasped.

"Yes, gold coins. If I had lots of gold coins, the villagers would be out here day and night, trying to borrow from me, trying to sell me things I don't want. And robbers would come. I would be scared and miserable. I want to live a quiet, simple life. No visitors—except, of course, for you. You are always welcome for tea."

The tengu grew sleepy by the fire and fell into a slumber. At dawn, he flew away. Immediately, the old woman bundled up and went into the forest. All day she cut bushes and brush. She hauled the branches back to her hut. She did not rest. By nightfall, her hut was covered, inside, outside, and on the roof—thorny thickets all around. She waited.

When night came, she heard a howling. It was the tengu. He had returned and found the brush stacked around her house. He could not fly near. "I'll get even with you, Granny!"

The old woman waited and waited. The howling resumed. "Now I'll fix you!" he cried out. Down her smoke hole dropped a small gold coin. Then another.

"Please, stop!" the old woman cried.

"Take this," the demon answered back and threw in more coins.

The old woman continued to scream in terror as she gathered up the gold coins. So many coins poured into her hut that she stood almost knee deep in gold.

The tengu shouted, "This is my final revenge." He dumped in

dozens of round, sweet cakes.

The old woman screamed louder, "Oh, no! Please don't scare me with dongo." Down the dongo rolled and bounced and covered the gold coins.

The tengu gave a mighty laugh and flew away, avenged.

The old woman gathered up the cakes and coins. She made tea and sat down to eat her favorite treat and count her money.

Years passed. The tengu never returned. And the old woman lived in comfort all her days.

Lydia Barrington Darragh
1729–1789

Lydia Darragh was an unlikely spy—a petite, prim, respectable Philadelphia housewife. But it was this very unlikeliness that helped her outwit the British Army.

In the fall of 1777, the British Army defeated the Revolutionary Army at the Battles of Brandywine and Germantown and then occupied Philadelphia. General Howe set up his headquarters in a house on Second Street. Lydia Darragh, a Quaker, lived across the street. The Peace Testimony of the Society of Friends forbade Quakers to take sides in the Revolutionary War. However, Lydia Darragh's son, Charles, was a Free Quaker who believed the patriot's cause was just. He joined the second Pennsylvania Regiment and was camped with General Washington nearby at Whitemarsh.

The British, needing additional housing for officers, ordered Darragh to move. She went to Lord Howe to personally ask for permission to remain in her house. On the way, she met a British officer, Captain Barrington, who turned out to be a second cousin. Barrington intervened on her behalf, and Darragh was allowed to stay in her house provided she kept a room available for British meetings.[1]

On December 2, an aide to General Howe notified Darragh that her back room was needed for an evening meeting. She and her family were asked to retire early. The aide said, "When the meeting is over, I will knock on your door and you may let us out, extinguish the fire, and lock the front door behind us."

That night she sent her family to bed. While the British convened, she took off her shoes and tiptoed to a linen closet next to the meeting room. Putting her ear to the thin wall, she heard the plans for a major offensive against Whitemarsh at midnight on December fourth. General Howe, acting on information from his spies, heard that the Americans were moving to a new camp. He wanted to catch the Americans out in the open.

After hearing all the details, Darragh went to her bed and feigned sleep. A British officer knocked on her door—once, twice...She did not respond. After the third knock, she rose and let the British out.[2]

The next morning Darragh told her family she needed to go to Frankfort for flour. She refused to take a servant. Because the mill was outside Philadelphia, Darragh had to obtain a pass to cross the British line. She traveled through the snow to the mill, left her bag, and went searching for a place to deliver her information.

Her destination was the Rising Sun Tavern, a meeting place for patriot spies. Inside the dark tavern, she spotted Colonel Craig of the Philadelphia Light Horse Troop, who served with her son.[3] Silently, she handed him "a dirty old needle book, with various small pockets in it." Inside was a rolled-up paper with information that General Howe was coming out that night with "5,000 men, 13 pieces of cannon, baggage wagons, and 11 boats on wheels."[4]

Colonel Craig took the news to General Washington; Darragh collected her flour and returned home. The British moved out at midnight. When they neared the American position, they saw innumerable campfires burning in the hills. They did not know that Washington had ordered his men to make extra campfires to fool the British as to their true numbers.

Washington sent out six hundred Pennsylvania militiamen to meet the Redcoats. In a brief engagement, the British fired, but instead of fighting, the Americans retreated to the hills. General Howe climbed a church tower to survey the American position. The American position, just half a mile away, was strongly defended.

After several days and several skirmishes, Howe lost heart for the fight. The American position was too strong and the weather was too cold. Thus, on the afternoon of December eighth, the British marched back to Philadelphia.

Obviously, somebody had leaked word to Washington, and the

British looked for the spy. Several suspects were questioned, including Lydia Darragh. On December ninth, General Howe's aide knocked on her door once more. He asked if anyone had been up on the night of December second. She replied that everyone went to sleep early. The aide believed her, remembering that he had had to knock three times to wake her. He left saying, "I am entirely at a loss to imagine who gave General Washington information of our intended attack, unless the walls of the house could speak. When we arrived near Whitemarsh, we found all their cannon mounted, and the troops prepared to receive us; and we have marched back like a parcel of fools."[5]

On December 11, Washington broke camp at Whitemarsh and headed to Valley Forge.

DEMANDING
OUR RIGHTS

Let us see what a few earnest, capable women can do.
—Belva Lockwood

The Daughters of Zelophehad

The Woman's Bible

Then came the daughters of Zelophehad, the son of Hepher, the son of Gilead, the son of Machir, the son of Manasseh, of the families of Manasseh, the son of Joseph; and these are the names of his daughters: Mahiah, Noah, and Hogiah, and Milcah, and Tirzah.

And they stood before Moses, and before Eleazar the priest, and before the princes and all the congregation, by the door of the tabernacle of the congregation, saying,

Our father died in the wilderness, and he was not in the company of them that gathered themselves together against the Lord in the company of Korah.

Why should the name of our father be done away from among his family, because he hath no son? Give us therefore a possession among the brethren of our father.

And Moses brought their cause before the Lord.

And the Lord spake unto Moses, saying,

The daughters of Zelophehad speak right: thou shalt surely give them a possession of an inheritance among their father's brethren and thou shalt cause the inheritance of their father to pass unto them.

And thou shalt speak unto the children of Israel, saying, If a man die, and have no son, then ye shall cause his inheritance to pass unto his daughter.

And if he have no daughter, then ye shall give his inheritance unto his brethren.

And if he have no brethren, then ye shall give his inheritance unto his father's brethren.

And if his father have no brethren, then ye shall give his inheritance unto his kinsman that is next to him of his family, and he shall possess it; and it shall be unto the children of Israel a statute of judgment, as the Lord commanded Moses.

Julia Smith and Abby Smith

1792–1886 and 1797–1878

In 1873, American women were gearing up to fight for their voting rights. Two sisters, Abby and Julia Smith, inspired other suffragists with a tax protest. It all had to do with seven cows, and this is how it happened.

Abby, seventy-seven, and Julia, eighty-two, were the last surviving of five daughters of an educated Connecticut family. In November 1873, the property tax on their family homestead in Glastonbury was increased by one hundred dollars. Only two parcels in town, owned by women, had been reassessed; the taxes of the voting males had remained unchanged.

The Smith sisters went to the next town meeting to protest. Abby delivered a spirited oration about taxation without representation; the men listened in chilly silence. At another meeting, five months later, when Abby was denied the right to speak, she climbed on a wagon outside the town hall and read her speech. The sisters refused to pay the tax.

In January 1874, the tax collector impounded seven cherished Smith cows for an unpaid tax bill of $101.39. The cows, who were housed at a neighbor's barn, refused to be milked and disturbed the village with their lowing. At auction, the sisters successfully bid for four cows before their money ran out. Jessie, Bessie, Whitney, and Minnie were saved from bondage; the other three were sold.[1]

The protest began to attract national attention. Abby's first speech was published in the *Hartford Courant;* newspapers across the country began to write stories about the "Glastonbury Cows." The *Springfield Republican* set up a defense fund. Souvenirs made from the cow's tails were sold in Chicago. Abby and Julia appeared at numerous suffrage conventions.[2]

Meantime, fifteen acres of the sisters' pastureland was seized for nonpayment of taxes. At the last minute, the location of the auction was shifted to prevent the Smiths from attending. A neighboring man bought the land—worth $2,000—for just $78.35.

The sisters sued the tax collector for violating a town law that land could not be taken before movable property. Several years, several trials, and several appeals later, the sisters prevailed. The other three cows were never recovered.

Later, Julia published the speeches and newspaper accounts in a pamphlet, *Abby Smith and Her Cows*. Isabella Beecher Hooker suggested the cow be adopted as the emblem for a suffrage banner. She said, "Abby Smith and her cows are marching on like John Brown's soul."[3]

LEAVING ABUSE BEHIND

On Saturday night I lost my wife,
And where do you think I found her?
Up in the moon, singing a tune,
And all the stars around her.
　　　—Mother Goose

Hina, the Woman in the Moon

Hawaii

All her life, Hina worked hard making tapa cloth. All day, year after year, she sat outside her house beating bark into thin sheets with her mallet. Every night, she carried water to the house and cooked the meals. Her bad-tempered husband did not help; he just demanded she work harder.

One day as she was beating bark into cloth, she cried out, "Oh, if only I could go where I can rest in my old age."

The Rainbow heard her cry and sent a path to her feet. She stepped on the arch. *I will climb to the Sun. There I will rest.*

Up and up. Closer and closer. The Sun's rays scorched her face and singed her hair. She dropped to her knees and crawled higher until she had no more strength. Hina slid down the Rainbow arch and came to earth again.

She lay exhausted until the sun set and darkness descended. The moon rose—full and cool and silent. She pulled herself up. *I will climb to the Moon. There I will rest.*

Hina went into her house to pack her favorite things—her tapa board and mallet. Her husband demanded, "Where are you going, old woman?"

She walked out the door and to the base of the Rainbow. "I am climbing to the Moon where I can rest," she declared.

He followed her. "Who will cook my meals and pound the cloth?"

She stepped on the arch and began to climb. Just when she was almost out of reach, he jumped and grabbed her foot. "You can't leave," he said. He slipped, twisting and breaking Hina's foot before he fell.

Hina climbed to the clouds, singing to the Stars through her pain: "Please, guide me." The Stars lit her way and the Moon gave her respite.

During a full moon, you can still see her there. She is sitting with her lame foot. Perhaps, if you see wispy fine clouds clustered around the Moon, it is the tapa cloth that Hina is beating.

Tina Turner

1939–

In 1956, seventeen-year-old Anna Mae Bullock grabbed a microphone in a St. Louis jazz spot, Club Manhattan. While Ike Turner played a B.B. King tune during intermission, Anna sang, "You Know I Love You." Ike ran to pick her up and said, "Giiirrrll! I didn't know you could really sing."[1]

Ike hired the singer from Nutbush, Tennessee, changed her name to Tina, dressed her in sequins, and took her on the road with the Kings of Rhythm. Two years later he married her in Tijuana. In October 1960, Ike's band became the Ike & Tina Turner Revue.

Offstage, Tina endured Ike's infidelities and beatings. "Yes, it finally got to point where I was ready to die. Ike was beating me with phones, with shoes, with hangers. Choking me, punching me—it wasn't just slapping anymore," she said.[2] On July 1, 1976, in a limousine going to a Dallas hotel, Ike backhanded her. She thought, "Today, I'm fighting back."[3]

As soon as Ike passed out in the hotel, Tina ran down the alley to a Ramada Inn. She had thirty-six cents and a Mobil credit card. Fortunately, the manager gave her a room for the night. Her life with Ike ended at that moment, and her new life began.

A conversion to Buddhism helped Tina find the strength to leave Ike and support their four sons. After depending on food stamps and friends, she recruited a band and played the cabaret circuit. She was almost forty.

The divorce was final in 1978. Tina renounced all her rights to their recording studio, real estate, and royalties. "My peace of mind was more important."[4] She kept the name Tina Turner.

In 1979, she caught the ear of manager Roger Davies, who promoted her comeback. In 1984, *Private Dancer* returned her to stardom; it sold more than ten million copies. The success continued with hits, tours, and awards.

Tina wrote her autobiography—*I, Tina*—which chronicled her abusive marriage. The book was the basis for the 1993 movie, *What's Love Got to Do With It*. Angela Bassett played Tina, but Tina sang the songs.

Meanwhile, Ike was serving eighteen months in prison for cocaine possession; after his release, he remarried and tried to resume his musical career.

He denied beating Tina. In a interview with *Jet* magazine, he said, "I slapped her. The only time I ever punched Tina with my fist was that last fight we had...All the times before that, our little slaps, or whatever they were, were all just about attitude." He said that he felt there was no other way to deal with Tina. "That's the only way. You don't get across to her no other kind of way."[5] After the release of *What's Love Got to Do With It*, Ike set up his own 900 telephone number to tell his side of the story.

Since 1986, the leggy Hanes spokesperson has lived in Switzerland with Erwin Bach, a German record company executive. Tina said, "I don't have a desire to marry. We are perfect just as we are. Besides, I want to keep my stuff mine and his stuff his. That's the reality. I need that freedom."[6]

PREDICTING
THE FUTURE

With these eight words the wiccan rede fulfill:
"An it harm none, do what ye will."
—The Wicca Creed

Biddy Early's Bottle

Ireland

Some folks called Biddy Early a healer; some called her a witch; W.B. Yeats called her "the wisest of wise women."

She was born Bridget Ellen Connors in 1798. She grew up a barefoot, red-haired farm girl in County Clare on the Emerald Isle. She had only two distinctions: she could read, and she knew the healing power of herbs.

Until she was widowed at twenty-three, Biddy Early was an ordinary farmer's wife. To support herself and her son Paddy, she made herb mixtures from family recipes and dispensed them to ill neighbors and their livestock. Her reputation as a healer became widespread. Although she had three more husbands, she called herself by her mother's surname—Early.

One day, Paddy—now a strapping teenager—was walking home along a country road. A group of the Good People were playing a swift game of hurling in a field. They waved to him. "Come join us."

He called back, "Thank you anyway, but I am on a trot to get back to my mom."

The wee men beckoned again, "Come and play; we're short a player. And we've heard that you're the finest hurler in these parts."

Well, Paddy couldn't resist the flattery or the chance to show his skill, so he jumped onto the field and seized a hurling stick. Soon he was scoring goals and playing the game of his life. After a long victorious battle, his team presented him with an empty, dark glass bottle.

"This bottle is our gift for such a fine game," they said. "Take it to your mother; she'll know what to do with it." The fairies jumped into the bushes, but before disappearing, they warned, "Tell her to take no money for her services—but she can accept gifts."

Paddy walked straight home and gave the bottle to his mother. She took it in her hands, turning it round and round. A mist filled the interior. "Oh, my," Biddy Early exclaimed as she saw figures and signs swirling in the mist, "this gift from the fairies will be my talisman."

Biddy Early now had two powers—healing and foretelling. When strangers showed up at her door for a cure, she greeted them by name. She knew intimate details of their lives; she could see and hear events far from her door.

When it suited her, Biddy Early predicted horse races. Once a race was going to be held just three miles from her cottage. A rich stranger, who fully intended to win, was bringing two horses, a chestnut and a bay, to the meet. When he neared the house of Biddy Early, he decided to stop and test her powers. He hid the horses down the road, knocked on the door, and was told to come in. "God be with the house," he said when he saw the seer sitting in her chair.

She cut short any pleasantries. "So you think the chestnut will win, do you? You're wrong, it'll be the bay."

The stranger was taken aback. How could she know his thoughts? Was all that he heard about her true? When he left, he dismissed her prophecy. After all, he knew his horses; the chestnut was the better horse.

He entered both horses in the race and bet heavily on his favorite. The chestnut never had a heart for the race, and the bay won easily. The stranger went home a wiser but poorer man.

Through the years, Biddy Early heeded the Good People's warning and never charged for her foretellings. Instead, she accepted fresh baked bread, tea and sugar, bottles of whiskey or poteen. Since she was not a drinking woman, most of the liquor passed to her husbands, which played havoc with their health. Biddy Early never became a rich woman, but she always shared what she had with the hungry travelers who came to her door.

The local clergy were in an uproar over the non-churchgoing, card-playing, often-married Biddy Early. The priests unsuccessfully commanded their parishioners not to seek cures from her. In 1865, she was charged with witchcraft under a 1586 statute. Her current husband drove her in a cart to the court in Ennis. No one would testify against her, and the case was dismissed for lack of evidence.

In 1874, Biddy Early lay dying and summoned a priest to give her last rites. Father Connellon, the parish priest from Freakle, heard her confession and gave her the sacrament of Extreme Unction. All the while, a crow kept flying against the window. The crow was let in and sat at the foot of the deathbed. Biddy Early gave her bottle to the priest. "'Tis for you now an' you'll have the same powers as I had."

When she died, the crow cawed and flew out the window. The priest took the dark fairy bottle and threw it into Kilbarron Lake. And since no one has ever found it, the bottle lies there still.

Zsuzsanna Emese Budapest

1940–

Zsuzsanna Emese Budapest, who likes to be called "Z," is credited with founding the contemporary Goddess movement known as Dianic Wicca, or Feminist Witchcraft. She was born in Budapest, Hungary, into a long line of witches. Her mother, Masika Szilagyi, a medium and a practicing witch, supported herself as a sculptress. Masika's themes always celebrated the Triple Goddess and the Fates.

When the revolution broke out in 1956, Z was one of sixty-five thousand political refugees who fled Hungary. She escaped on foot through the swamps to Austria where she took the name Zsuzsanna Budapest. In 1959, Budapest emigrated to the United States; in Chicago she married, gave birth to two sons, and practiced solo worship of the Goddess at her home altar.

After a divorce, Budapest moved to southern California and joined the women's liberation movement. She observed that the feminist movement lacked spirituality. "Without the Goddess, feminism is not going to work, because you're going to burn out."[1] She founded the Susan B. Anthony Coven Number l, the first feminist witches' coven. Dianic Witchcraft is a for-women-only, Goddess-centered religion with roots in the early pagan religions of Europe.

In 1975, she opened a candle shop, The Feminist Wicca, and began reading tarot cards for customers. Fortunetelling was against a local law which was only sporadically enforced.

One day an undercover policewoman came in for a reading. "Suddenly there was an intense smell of cat shit," Budapest recalls.[2] Instinctively she knew something was wrong and tried to reschedule, but the policewoman pressed her for a reading.

Budapest turned over the first card, the one representing the policewoman; it was the devil. One of the meanings of the devil card is bondage. She inquired, "Do you work in places where you feel tied down, or where there are other people who have been restricted?"[3]

After the reading was over, two policemen entered the store and arrested her. She called out a curse to the policeman who pulled out a pair of handcuffs: "Four months of bad dreams to the first man who touches me!" [4] The men did not cuff her.

Budapest's defense at trial was that, as a witch, fortunetelling was her religious right. While women picketed with signs reading NO MORE WITCH TRIALS outside a municipal court in west Los Angeles, other witches, an anthropologist, even a Christian priest testified that Budapest had simply been practicing her religion. The jury found her guilty. She filed several appeals but never won a reversal. In 1985, the California Supreme court struck down the law against fortunetelling.[5]

Currently, Budapest lives in the San Francisco Bay Area, operates a 900 number—"The Goddess Hotline"—and gives workshops and lectures. She is the author of *The Holy Book of Women's Mysteries, The Grandmother of Time, Grandmother Moon, The Goddess in the Office* and *The Goddess in the Bedroom,* and *Summoning the Fates: A Woman's Guide to Destiny.*

SAVORING LIFE

Everything in excess.
To enjoy the flavor of life, take big bites.
Moderation is for monks.
     —Robert A. Heinlein, *Time Enough for Love*

Clever Gretel

Germany

There was a cook named Gretel. She wore shoes with red heels. When she went walking in those shoes, she turned herself this way and that. "Gretel, you are a clever creature, you are!" she would say to herself.

When she went back to her master's house, she always took a little sip of wine. "Wine sharpens the tongue," she would say. "And what's a cook without a tongue to taste?" In fact, Gretel kept her tongue very busy, nibbling and sampling.

Now one day her master said to her: "I have a guest coming this evening, Gretel, and a guest that knows what's what. I want you to cook us a pair of hens. And I want them roasted to a turn."

Gretel picked up her cleaver. "Yes, master. Your wish is my command."

So she killed two chickens, scalded and plucked them, stuffed them, stuck them on a spit, and put them over red coals to roast. She turned them and turned them. Her round cheeks were red from the fire.

She had a little sip of wine. "I'm so thirsty from the heat." She had another sip and then another.

She basted the birds and basted them. When they were done to a turn, Gretel called out, "If that guest of yours doesn't come soon, master, I'll have to take the birds away from the fire. And it's a shame for they are just at their juiciest."

Her master ran to the front doorstep. "I'll see if he is coming."

Gretel peered out of the window. When she saw no one, she glanced at the hens. "I wonder if these birds taste as good as they smell." A tiny scrap of skin dropped on the coals. Gretel scooped it into her mouth. "Perfection."

A wing flared up. "There! What did I tell you? One of the wings is burning." She cut the wing with a twist of her sharp knife and ate every morsel.

She studied the chicken. "With one wing left, it looks out of kilter!" So she ate up the other wing. Then she took another sip of wine.

"What a sad thing," she said. "Once those two poor hens were twins, and you couldn't tell 'em apart. But now look at them; one with wings sticking up and one with no wings at all." So she gobbled up the wings of the other chicken to make the pair look more alike. And still the guest did not arrive.

She shrugged her shoulders. "Gretel, my dear, there'll be no guest tonight. He has forgotten all about it. It's a pity for his bird to go to waste." So she ate up one of the hens—skin, stuffing, gravy, and all.

How sad and lonely the other looked—all by itself with its legs sticking up in the air and both its wings gone. She finished it off, too. "The master can have some nice bread and cheese."

She was picking the very last sweet slivers off the wishbones when her master came running into the kitchen. "Quick, Gretel! Dish up! Our guest is coming down the road."

At that moment, she was facing the fire, in her fine shoes and great cooking apron. She looked over her shoulder in surprise. Her master did not notice the grease on her face; instead, he snatched up the carving knife and stone and ran to the front doorstep.

Soon, the guest came round to the kitchen door and knocked. "I'm sorry I'm late."

"Hush." Gretel put her finger to her lips, and whispered, "My master has gone mad from your tardiness. Listen now! He's at the front door sharpening his knife. If he catches you, he will cut off your ears."

When the guest heard the rasping of the knife on the stone, he turned pale.

"Run!" said Gretel.

And run he did—down the street as fast as his legs could carry him. As soon as he was out of sight, Gretel wiped the grease from her chin.

She hastened out to her master. "Sir, what kind of a guest did you ask to supper?"

"What's wrong with him?" said he.

"Wrong!" said she. "Why, he put his nose into the kitchen and took a sniff. Then he dashed in and snatched up your two fine hens. He ran off down the street with one under each arm."

"When?"

"Now!"

The master cried, "Then I shall have nothing for supper but bread and cheese!" And out he ran after the guest. "Stop! Give me one! Just one!"

The guest saw his host and his sharp knife and thought the madman wanted one of his ears. He ran faster than ever into the darkness of the night.

Gretel went back to the kitchen and sat down in her rocker. She gave a contented sigh, admired her shoes with the red heels, and took another sip. "Gretel, you are a clever creature, you are!"

Alice B. Toklas

1877–1967

In 1907, Alice Toklas, the daughter of a prosperous San Francisco family, traveled to Paris and met Gertrude Stein. For the next forty years, Toklas and Stein shared a studio at 27 rue de Fleurus. Paintings by Renoir, Matisse, and Picasso covered their walls.[1]

"Lovey" and "Pussy," as they called each other, presided over a salon of intellectual expatriates called "the lost generation."[2] On Saturday nights, Toklas cooked copious amounts of free food such as "Bass for Picasso" and "Custard Josephine Baker." Gourmet James Beard said, "Alice was one of the great cooks of all time."[3]

In 1954, Toklas wrote *The Alice B. Toklas Cookbook*. Although it included recipes for traditional French dishes, her book is best remembered for the recipe for *Haschich Fudge:* pulverized *cannabis sativa* mixed with chopped dates, figs, nuts, and spices. She commented this "food of Paradise" might provide an "entertaining refreshment for the Ladies' Bridge Club or a chapter meeting of the DAR."[4]

In Chapter Ten of the cookbook, "Servants in France," Toklas remarked, "Unfortunately there have been too many of them in my service." Some of those servants had unusual reasons for leaving.[5] One cook named Louise asked to eat her meals before she served guests. This custom caused no trouble until an American family visited for Thanksgiving. While Toklas put a final basting on an imposing bird, the cook came to the oven with a carving knife and fork. Louise said a wing or a second joint should be sufficiently cooked for her to eat her portion at once. Toklas explained that "the turkey would not be presented and carved at table with even a small amputation." Louise threw her knife and fork on the table, burst into tears, and quit on the spot.[6]

Or perhaps the servant's name was not really Louise but Clever Gretel!

CASTING
A SPELL

Yet mark'd I where the bolt of Cupid fell
It fell upon a little western flower,
Before milk-white, now purple with love's wound,
And maidens call it love-in-idleness.
Fetch me that flower; the herb I shew'd thee once:
The juice of it on sleeping eye-lids laid
Will make man or woman madly dote
Upon the next live creature that it sees.
—Shakespeare, *A Midsummer Night's Dream*

Br'er Rabbit and Mammy-Bammy Big-Money

United States

Mammy-Bammy Big-Money, the Witch-Rabbit, lived way off in a dark swamp. To get there Br'er Rabbit had to ride some, slide some, hop some, flop some, creep some, sleep some. And if he wasn't monstrous careful, he wasn't going to get there at all.

He arrived all worn out and out of breath, so he sat down to rest. He saw black smoke coming out of a hole in the ground. *That must be where the old Witch-Rabbit lives*, he thought.

He called out in a small, trembly voice: "Mammy-Bammy Big-Money, I need your help."

No answer. The smoke just poured out blacker.

He called out louder, "Mammy-Bammy Big-Money, I need your help."

No answer, but the smoke just poured out blacker.

Br'er Rabbit called out in a bigger, tremblier voice, "Mammy-Bammy Big-Money, I need your help!"

And out of the hole, a loud, hoarse voice replied, "Why so, Br'er Rabbit? Why so?"

"Mammy-Bammy Big-Money, I need a charm bag."

The big voice asked again, "Why so, Br'er Rabbit? Why so?"

"I'm in love, Mammy-Bammy Big-Money. I'm in love."

"Well, you do need my help, you can't get a girl without a charm bag. You must bring me three things; first, bring me an elephant tusk."

Br'er Rabbit was so happy to be getting his charm bag, he ran, he jumped, and he cracked his heels. The next day he saw a great big elephant breaking his way through the woods.

"My," said Br'er Rabbit, "you're a big elephant for true. But you are so big, you can't be very strong."

"See this!" Elephant said. He took a pine tree in his trunk and pulled it up by the roots.

Br'er Rabbit said, "You pulled up that little sapling because you are so tall, not because you are so strong. See that big pine there. You can't pull it up."

Elephant answered back, "See this!"

Elephant charged at the big pine and tried to pull it up with his trunk, but the tree was too tough for him. He stuck his tusk in the tree and tried to pull it up. The big pine tree was too tough for true, and the tusk broke off. B'er Rabbit unstuck that tusk and took it to the witch-woman.

Br'er Rabbit said, "Elephant is too big to be smart."

Mammy-Bammy Big-Money said, "Now, you must have one gator tooth to go with the elephant tusk."

Br'er Rabbit cracked his heels; he traveled long on a dusty, hot, and bumpy road until he met a gator. He said, "This road is so dusty, hot, and bumpy. Let's make a nice, smooth one by the creek-side."

The gator liked the idea of a new road. Gator cleared the brush with his teeth. He swept the trash away with his tail.

Br'er Rabbit beat the bushes down with his cane. He hit left. He hit right. He hit up. He hit down. He hit all around. He hit and he hit until by and by, he hit Gator in the mouth. He knocked out a tooth and grabbed it up. He was gone!

When Br'er Rabbit gave Mammy-Bammy Big-Money the gator tooth, she said, "This is one sharp tooth for true. Now fetch me a rice-bird bill."

Br'er Rabbit clicked his heels and he traveled far. He traveled far, until he saw a rice-bird swinging on a bush. He asked the bird, "Can you fly?"

"Surely!" Rice-bird said. He whistled; he sang; he shook his wing and he flew round and round and landed.

Br'er Rabbit said, "Surely you fly when the wind is blowing. Can you fly when the wind is not blowing?"

"Surely," Rice-bird said.

"Then fly in the house where there is no wind."

Rice-bird whistled; he sang; he shook his wings and he flew into the house. Br'er Rabbit pulled the door shut, he looked at the rice-bird, and he said, "Surely!"

Quick-quick, Br'er Rabbit caught the bird and took his bill. Quick-quick Br'er Rabbit took it to the Witch-Rabbit. She said, "This rice-bird bill is slick for true." She put the elephant tusk, the gator tooth, and the rice-bird bill into a little bag. She swung that bag over Br'er Rabbit's neck.

Mammy-Bammy Big-Money said, "Now you can marry that young gal. Surely."

Did Br'er Rabbit win the heart of the girl with his charm bag?

Did he make her his wife?

That's another story.

Marie Laveau

ca. 1794–1881

The name of Marie Laveau is associated with voodoo in New Orleans. There were two Marie Laveaus. The first Laveau was hailed both as a voodoo queen and saintly benefactor. Her less influential and more malevolent daughter was Marie Laveau II (1827–1897). Mother and daughter were almost identical in appearance: tall, statuesque, with black curly hair wrapped in a *tignon,* or kerchief, tied in seven knots and clasped with jewels.[1] History and folklore have frequently confused the two women.

Many of the details about Marie Laveau I's life are disputed; the accounts are a mixture of fact, fiction, and exaggeration. She was born in New Orleans, a free woman of black, white, and Indian blood. Reputedly, she was the daughter of Charles Laveau, a plantation owner, and Marguerite Carcantel, a petite black woman.

In 1819, she married Jacques Paris, a quadroon (three-fourths white, one-fourth black) from what is present-day Haiti. Paris disappeared and Laveau I supported herself as a hairdresser to wealthy white and Creole women. She gathered confidences and secrets from her clients which she later used to win influence among the elite.

Around 1826, Laveau established a relationship with another Haitian quadroon, Louis Christophe Duminy de Glapion. They never married but had fifteen children. Laveau quit hairdressing to devote all her time to the practice of voodoo.

Many rival voodoo queens fought for the lucrative business of selling charms and curses, but Laveau became the most popular. She used a combination of voodoo, theater, and Catholic practices to gain power, prestige, and money. She gained control of the dances held in Congo Square, a field near Orleans and Rampart Streets. On Sundays, slaves were allowed to dance and drum in the field. Tourists paid admission to see Laveau, dressed as a gypsy, dance with her twenty-foot snake, Zombie.[2]

She also presided over rites at Bayou St. John on the shore of Lake Pontchartrain. One of the most important events occurred every June 23, St. John's Eve. She would rise out of the lake, holding a burning candle in each hand and balancing a burning communion candle on her head. While drums played, she would walk across the water and begin the voodoo rites, perhaps praying over a black coffin or sacrificing roosters. When the ceremony was over, she would walk back across the water and disappear into the lake.[3]

She dealt in love charms and *gris-gris* (little bags containing herbs and natural matter, such as powdered brick, fingernail clippings, or hair). The bag, which could bring intended good luck or bad, was worn around the neck or left near the intended object.[4]

One widely circulated story about her magic concerned a wealthy young Creole charged with raping a young woman from a good family. His father hired the best attorneys but they had little hope of acquittal. The father offered Laveau a handsome reward if his son were released.

At dawn on the day of the trial, Laveau visited St. Louis Cathedral. She spent the morning in prayer at the altar rail while holding three guinea peppers in her mouth. Leaving the church, she entered the Cabildo, the seat of government and courthouse adjacent to the Cathedral. After persuading a worker to give her access to the empty courtroom, the voodoo queen hid the guinea peppers under the judge's chair and departed.

The evidence was strongly against the defendant, but the jury was reportedly composed of young Creole playboys. Although the jury deliberations were lengthy, the verdict was "not guilty." The grateful father gave Laveau the deed to a small cottage in the French Quarter, on St. Anne Street.[5]

The drama continued when the exonerated young man began going to church to say prayers of gratitude for his acquittal. He repented his decadent ways and decided to marry the young woman he had wronged. When the young man was spurned, he turned to Laveau also. She filled a gris-gris bag with love powder, feathers, ground lizard eggs, and donkey hair and told the lover to wear it around his waist. She then sprinkled bits of his hair on the young woman's doorstep.

The young woman encountered her suitor as she was leaving church. She ran from him, fell, and sprained her ankle. The young man picked her up and treated her so tenderly that she allowed him to kiss her. They wed the next day.[6]

Laveau lived in the St. Anne Street house until her death. The obituaries neglected to mention her voodoo practices and instead praised her benevolent care of the victims of the yellow fever epidemic in the 1850s and her ministrations to death-row inmates. She is reportedly buried in the family tomb at St. Louis Cemetery No. 1. There is a question whether Laveau or her daughter is buried in this raised tomb, which is marked MARIE PHILOME GLAPION.[7]

The New Orleans Voodoo Museum leads a walking tour to the cemetery and recommends making a wish on the tomb.[8] Visitors, who seek favors, make red chalk X's on the face of the tomb and leave offerings of food, flowers, and candles. So popular is the tomb that a picture of it appears on the Internet with instructions for making a love wish.[9]

Perhaps Laveau isn't buried any place; legend holds that she never died but changed herself into a big black crow that flies over the cemetery. The bird's feathers stick out and resemble the kerchief Laveau wore, tied in seven knots around her head.[10]

AGITATING FOR THE WORKERS

Us kids worked twelve hours a day.
For fourteen cents of measly pay.
It's hard times, cotton mill girls.
It's hard times everywhere.
            —American folksong "Cotton Mill Girls"

The Gypsy Woman
England

Do you remember the story of Tom Tit Tom? It's the English version of Rumpelstiltskin. The king married a poor woman's daughter because he thought she could spin five skeins of flax a day. "For eleven months out of the year she shall have all she likes to eat and all the gowns she likes to wear," he said, "but the last month of the year she'll have to spin five skeins a day. If she doesn't, I shall kill her."

But it was Tom Tit Tom who did the spinning. You might have thought the queen lived happily ever after when she guessed Tom Tit Tom's name. She said, "I bet the king will forget all about the spinning next year."

But the king did not forget. "Wife," he said, "eleven months are up; beginning tomorrow you must spin five skeins a day for a month."

The poor queen, who could not spin at all, asked him, "What will happen if I don't spin five skeins a day?"

"Why, my dear, I'll have your head. That's the bargain. But that won't happen; these pretty little fingers will make fast work of that flax," said the king as he kissed each fingertip.

When the queen fled to her room, she collapsed into tears—tears for the throne she would lose, tears for the husband she would lose, tears for the head she would lose.

The sound of the queen's sobs carried across the courtyard. Out of the shadows stepped a woman in a dark cloak. The woman walked to the balcony and threw back her hood. The moonlight shone on the beautiful face of a gypsy. "My queen, the salt from your tears stings my soul. Can I help you?"

"No one can help me. I'll be be put to death for deceiving the king." The queen brightened. "Do you know Tom Tit Tom? Can you bring him to me?"

"No, my queen, I do not know this man."

"Then can you spin five skeins a day?"

The gypsy laughed. "If I could, I would be rich and I wouldn't be wearing this shabby cloak. Tell me your story and perhaps I can think of a clever solution."

The queen, in her desperation, told the whole story. She concluded, "And I should tell him the truth, but I don't know if he loves me or the work he thinks I can do."

"I will help. First you must persuade the king to host a party tomorrow night before you are locked away. Second, you must give me a gown and jewels to wear to the party."

The queen threw open her wardrobe. Out spilled gowns of every hue. "Take what you want."

The gypsy stood before a mirror and held up gown after gown. At last she chose a gown of crimson velvet.

"Oh, not that one," cried the queen. "It's my favorite." She thought a moment and said, "No—take it. The king has never seen it and will not recognize it as mine." Then she piled ropes and ropes of rubies into the gypsy's hand.

The gypsy was out the door and over the balcony. "I'll be back tomorrow night; all is well." She disappeared into the night.

The next day the queen implored the king, "Let me have a party tonight—just a little gaiety before I am locked away."

"Of course, my dear," said the king. "Have your party. But at midnight, you must begin to spin."

While the queen prepared for the party, she saw the servants carrying the slender flax stems, spindle, and spinning wheel to the tower room.

That night, music and friends filled the Great Hall. The queen did not dance; she sat watching for the beautiful gypsy. The minutes passed; the hours passed. "I was a fool to hope, a fool to trust," she said to herself.

At midnight, the musicians signaled the last dance. The king took the queen by her hand and led her into the circle. The dancers moved slowly around the room, hand over hand.

Suddenly, out of nowhere, the gypsy appeared in the chain. She winked a quick wink at the queen. The music sped up, and the dancers quickened into a skip. With a squeeze of the hand, the gypsy danced past the queen. The music sped up and the circle swirled faster. Breathless dancers dropped out until only the gypsy remained—whirling and stamping and clapping, her rubies catching the light of the fire.

Over the sound of the drums, a woman cried out, "My dress! Who soiled my dress?" She pointed to a long dark stain on her skirt.

"My coat! Who ruined my coat?" A man displayed a greasy spot. One by one all the dancers found marks on their clothes, arms and faces.

When the king spied a spot on his hand, he silenced the music. "Who is responsible for this?"

"I am, my lord." The gypsy fell to her knees in front of the king.

"Explain!" commanded the king.

"Forgive me," said the gypsy. "I have a great gift: I can spin five skeins a day. But it is also a great curse. While I spin, spindle grease covers my hands." She held up her palms, slick with a sooty, sticky oil. "It soaks into my skin, no matter how hard I wash. It covers everything I touch."

The king looked in horror at the gypsy's hands and then at his wife's small hands. He called for the footmen. "Go to the tower room and bring me the spindle and spinning wheel." When they were delivered, the king broke the wheel over his knee and threw it into the fire. "That's the end of that!" he said. "She'll spin no more—or I'll have her head."

When the guests were leaving, the gypsy came forward, wrapped in her cloak. She gave the queen a crimson velvet bundle tied with the rope of rubies. "Here's your gown. Not a spot on it. There's a small tin of axle grease in the pocket—in case you ever need it."

And so, the king and queen lived happily ever after . . . or like you and me, they lived many years and most of them were happy.

Sarah G. Bagley
?–ca. 1847

In most preindustrial cultures women made the clothing; the word *distaff,* a stick that holds the wool for spinning, has come to connote women's work or the female sex. Up until the nineteenth century in America, enslaved African women picked cotton in the fields and most women spun and wove in their houses. Gradually, the making of cloth changed from homespun to manufactured cloth; some women spun yarn at home and traded for cloth, others bought factory yarn to spin at home.[1] The factory production of cloth signaled the beginning of the Industrial Revolution.

In 1814, cotton mills were opened in Waltham, Massachusetts, but the site lacked water power. Textile manufacturers purchased land near Pawtucket Falls, on the Merrimack River, to build the first planned manufacturing town. The town was named Lowell, after Francis Cabot Lowell, the originator of the "Lowell Factory System." Lowell was to be a model city and avoid the harsh conditions found in the English textile cities.

The Lowell Factory System produced textiles under one roof, from raw material to finished cloth. The system also provided a reliable work force by recruiting young women from New England farms and small towns. Young women were viewed as cheaper and more compliant employees than men.

Strict rules governed the "mill girls," both inside and outside of work. The mill owner set up boardinghouses, usually run by respectable widows, who provided meals and supervision. The women paid $1.25 of their $1.75 weekly salary for room and board. They were required to attend a church of their choice. The women were expected to work only for two or three years and return to their families. Many banked their earnings to support widowed mothers or sent their brothers to college.

The women worked from five A.M. to seven P.M. with a half-hour for breakfast and dinner. Girls as young as ten years of age worked in the spinning room as "doffers," taking off the full bobbins and replacing them with empty ones.[2]

The working conditions were not ideal in this supposed model town, and from the beginning, the labor force hinted of unrest. In the 1830s, the women stopped work—or "turned out"—to protest increases in room and board rates. The City of Spindles expanded to eight mills, employing seven thousand people. More automated machines were installed in the mills. Women, who had previously tended two machines, were assigned four or five machines. The managers ordered "speed-ups" in the machines, lengthened workdays, and raised boardinghouse fees—without paying higher wages.

In 1844, Sarah Bagley, a mill worker from New Hampshire, led an organized labor protest called the Ten Hour Movement. Bagley, who went to work at Hamilton Mills in 1836, organized five hundred workers into the Lowell Female Labor Reform Association (LFLRA). Her objective was to have the Massachusetts legislature investigate conditions at the mills. She collected two thousand signatures for a law limiting the workday to ten hours. Leading a five-member delegation, Bagley testified before the legislature regarding mill conditions. The legislature declined to take action.[3]

After defeat, the LFLRA joined with the New England Workingmen's Association; Bagley developed a "female department," under the slogan "As is Woman, so is the Race." Next, Bagley campaigned against a local legislator who had rejected the ten-hour day. When the legislator was forced from office, he alleged that Bagley was linked with the corruption of a male union member. The wrongly accused Bagley quit the mill for the good of the union.[4]

Bagley became superintendent of the Lowell telegraph office and was the nation's first female telegraph operator, receiving between $300 and $500 a year.[5] After 1847, history has no record of her. But she had opened up a new career for women. By 1863, fifty women were employed by one telegraph line alone.[6]

In the mills, Yankee women left because of worsening work conditions, more accidents, and brown lung disease, caused by long-term inhalation of cotton. An abundance of Irish immigrants, desperate for work, took the jobs. Later, French Canadian, Polish, Portuguese, and Greek immigrants sought work in Lowell. Unlike the Yankee farm girls who worked for two or three years and lived in dormitories, these immigrants were permanent workers who lived in family groups. The model industrial town deteriorated into a slum.

BEFRIENDING
FELINES

The dog for the man, the cat for the woman.
—English proverb

Why Cat Lives with Woman

Africa

Once upon a time, Cat lived all by herself in the jungle. She was tired of being alone and frightened, so she took herself a companion—another cat.

One day as they walked on a path, they heard a rustle in the tall grass. Out pounced Leopard with a growl. So strong and swift was Leopard that the companion cat ran into the jungle and was never seen again.

So Cat went to live with Leopard. *He's the bravest animal in the jungle,* Cat thought. *And he has handsome spots.*

One day as Cat and Leopard walked on the path, they heard a rustle in the tall grass. Out leapt Lion with a roar. So large and fierce was Lion that Leopard ran into the jungle and was never seen again.

So Cat went to live with Lion. *He's the bravest animal in the jungle,* Cat thought. *And he has a handsome mane.*

One day as Cat and Lion walked on the path, they heard a rustle in the tall grass. Out charged Elephant with a trumpet. So tall and wide was Elephant that Lion ran into the jungle and was never seen again.

So Cat went to live with Elephant. *He's the bravest animal in the jungle,* Cat thought. *And he has handsome tusks.*

One day as Cat and Elephant walked on the path, they heard a rustle in the tall grass. Out sneaked Man with a long rifle. So dangerous and frightening was Man and his gun that Elephant ran into the jungle and was never seen again.

I will go live with Man, said Cat. *He's the bravest animal in the jungle. And he has a big gun.*

So Cat walked along the path with Man to a hut. Out walked Woman with a big club. "Where have you been and what food have you brought from your hunt?" asked Woman. So loud and angry was Woman that Man ran into the jungle.

I will live with woman, said Cat. *She is the bravest animal in the jungle.* So Cat moved in and has been with Woman to this very day.

Mabel Stark

1892–?

Mabel Stark was the first woman to train tigers for the circus; tigers had traditionally been considered too dangerous to be handled by women. When Stark graduated from nursing school in 1911, she went to California for a vacation. On her first night in Los Angeles, she met the manager of the Al G. Barnes Circus. She told him of her dream of becoming an animal trainer; the next day she was working for the circus as the assistant to the lion trainer.

Gradually, she developed her own tiger act and became known as the "Tiger Woman." Fred Bradna, the stage manager and master of ceremonies for the Ringling Brothers–Barnum & Bailey Circus, said, "No one else ever gave the Big Cage such a feeling of suspense in the presence of jungle beasts, and the novelty of a woman trainer enhanced her reception."[1] Stark inspired Mae West to write a movie, *I'm No Angel,* in which West played a lion trainer who worked for the "Big Show." The women resembled each other with their diminutive statures and platinum blonde hair; however, Mabel had a boyish slender build unlike Mae's hourglass figure.

Stark controlled the animals with her attitude and voice. She said, "The first lesson the tiger must learn is that he has a master who cannot be bluffed or intimidated." Stark did not use violence in training. "They can be subdued but never conquered, except by love. And that is the secret of all successful animal training."[2] At her peak, Stark worked alone in a cage with twelve Bengal tigers and a black panther. She entered the cage without a whip, gun, or iron fork. "I like facing them with just a stick and a revolver loaded with blank cartridges."[3]

One of her favorite tigers was Rajah. The cub, who had almost been crushed by its mother, was hand-raised by Stark while she was with the Barnes show. He slept under her covers on cold nights and walked on a jeweled harness. When Rajah was full-grown, she put him in the act and he created a sensation by wrestling with her. He sprang from his seat, stood on his hind legs, and put his forefeet around her neck. Stark threw the tiger to the ground and they rolled three or four times. No one had ever wrestled a tiger. She was forced to leave Rajah behind when she joined the Ringling Brothers–Barnum & Bailey Circus in 1922.

Stark said, "I love these big cats as a mother loves her children."[4] Occasionally the cats expressed their love for her. One day, during a performance, she was with a lion in an elevator cage, riding to the top of the tent. A piece of rigging fell on Stark's head and drew blood. Since cats are said to erupt into rages at sudden noises and surprises, Stark was in danger of being attacked as the blood flowed from the gash on her head. She could not escape since the cage was suspended forty feet in the air. As the cage descended, the lion, gentle and solicitous, licked her wound as if stanching the gush of blood from its own cub.[5]

However, in working with the big cats for more than twenty-five years, Stark was attacked repeatedly during training and performances; she trained them, not tamed them. When she was once asked what it took to be a tiger trainer, she thrust both legs from under her gown. "This," she said. Her legs were covered with scars. Indeed, her entire body was scarred where the tigers had clawed her.[6]

TAKING
A GAMBLE

Time and trouble may tame a wild young woman, but a wild old woman is uncontrollable by any force.
    —popular saying

The Bucca-Boo

Wales

There is a story about an old woman, more than four-score years, who lived in the Welsh countryside with her son and daughter-in-law. The old woman loved to play cards; in spite of wind or weather, she walked a mile or two to the village to indulge in her pleasure. With a crowd of like-minded people, she spent nights pitching pennies in the pot and calling for a better deal. At dawn, she reeled back over the stile, full of toddy and songs.

Her daughter-in-law, raised on prunes and proverbs, harped at her husband. "Do something about your mother; she's bringing us shame."

Her son put on a stern face. "Mom, at your time of life, you belong home at night."

"There'll be time enough for the rocker when I'm old," the old woman replied as she pulled on her hat and coat.

Her daughter-in-law lectured her like a child. "If you don't stop, the bucca-boo will carry you off."

"Buccas don't frighten me—neither the black nor white." She slammed the door behind her. "I don't believe in ghosts."

That very night, the daughter-in-law draped her husband in a white bedsheet. She led him to the stile where the old woman passed over. "Hide in the bushes. When your mom comes, spring out at her and wave your arms. She'll think you're the white bucca

161

out to grab her. She won't go out at night again."

The son crouched in the bushes while the wind howled around him. He jumped every time the branches rustled. He thought about the black bucca with its long claws and pointed teeth.

At last the old woman came along the path. As she neared the stile, she spotted a figure draped in a white sheet, wearing her son's boots. He leaped from the bushes and groaned.

The old woman looked at him over the fence. "Well, it's the meek little white bucca. You'd better scoot before the big bad black bucca arrives."

Her son gave another small groan.

She climbed on top of the stile and looked back over her shoulder. "On this dark night there's nought to see but the black bucca chasing me."

Her son gave a small squeak.

"It's coming, it's coming," she called. "It's here."

He gathered the sheet up over his knees and began to run. The briars caught the sheet. "The bucca has me!" he cried.

"Run!" the old woman cheered. "Run, run, run!"

Run he did—as fast as he could lay feet to the ground. And the old woman stood on the top of the stile and laughed and laughed.

When she entered the house, her son was in a faint in the rocking chair. The wife was wiping his sweaty face with the tattered sheet.

"Ta," said the old woman as she climbed the stairs to bed. "No use rubbing it in," she thought.

From that night to this, the old woman comes and goes as she pleases. Her son and daughter-in-law say no more about gambling or the buccas—black or white.

Poker Alice

1851–1930

Sometimes Lady Luck deals a full house and sometimes she deals a pair of deuces; that's the way it was for Alice Ivers, better known as Poker Alice. Sometimes her winnings brought her extravagant gowns from New York City, and sometimes her losses put her in army-surplus clothes. Poker Alice figured that half a million dollars passed through her fingers, "but very little stuck."[1]

Born in England, she immigrated to the western United States with her parents. She married a mining engineer and moved to Lake City, Colorado. The mountain mining town consisted of thirteen log cabins, many of them gambling halls. After her husband died in a dynamite explosion, poker-faced Alice earned her way as a professional gambler and dealer.

Poker Alice gambled in Oklahoma, Kansas, New Mexico, and Arizona. In her younger days, with her English accent and fashionable gowns, she was a frontier legend. She refused to gamble or drink on Sundays and regularly quoted the Bible. By midlife, Poker Alice smoked black cigars and carried a gun. She had become a frontier character.

At the age of fifty-six, after thirty years of the gambling life, she married a rival dealer, W.G. Tubbs, and settled happily on a South Dakota homestead. During their third winter, Tubbs died of pneumonia. Poker Alice was snowbound with his frozen body until the spring thaw. She pawned her wedding ring to pay for his funeral, then redeemed it with gambling winnings.

The widow opened a gambling joint in Sturgis, South Dakota, complete with women to entertain the soldiers from a nearby army post. One night, she killed a brawling soldier but pleaded the shooting was accidental. She read her Bible in jail while awaiting the verdict: not guilty by reason of self-defense.[2]

But Poker Alice was on a losing streak. She married and buried a third husband. She was arrested and convicted of "running a disorderly house." Although pardoned by the governor, she retired to raise chickens. She died in Sturgis at the age of seventy-nine and was buried in the St. Francis Cemetery. Her tombstone read:

"POKER ALICE," ALICE HUCKERT TUBBS
Feb. 17, 1851—Feb. 27, 1930[3]

Her headstone could have read:

SHE SAT DOWN AT THE TABLE,
ANTED UP,
AND PLAYED THE CARDS SHE WAS DEALT.

LIVING A
LONG LIFE

Some people don't want to get old.
Some people don't want to die.
You've got to do one or the other.
—Gail Sheehy, *New Passages*

Aunt Misery

Puerto Rico

Dear amigos, this is a tale about an old, old woman, living all alone, with not even a dog for company. The bully boys of the neighborhood were mean to her. They wanted to steal the fruit out of the pear tree that grew outside her hut. When the old woman chased them away, they called her crazy, they called her witch, they called her "Aunt Misery." She might have given them some juicy pears if they had asked nicely.

One day a traveler stopped by Aunt Misery's hut. "I am thirsty, hungry, and tired. Can you help me please?"

Aunt Misery fetched the traveler a dipper of cool water and a basket of ripe pears. "You may sleep by the woodpile tonight."

The next morning, the traveler said, "For your kindness, I will grant you one wish."

Aunt Misery didn't take the offer seriously. She just called out, "If anyone climbs my pear tree, I wish to keep them there until I let them go."

"Your wish is granted," said the traveler as he left.

Soon after, that gang of boys arrived with empty baskets. It looked like they intended to harvest all the pears. Three boys climbed up the tree. As they filled the baskets, they taunted Aunt Misery. She came out of her hut and stood patiently. When their baskets were full, the boys tried to climb down; they were stuck. Her wish had been granted.

"Please let us down," cried the boys. "We'll give you back your pears." They stayed stuck.

"Please let us down and we'll bring you fresh eggs!" the boys begged. They stayed stuck.

"Please let us down and we'll bring you the hen!" the boys pleaded. They stayed stuck.

Finally Aunt Misery had her fill of seeing the bullies squirm. "I'll let you go if you promise never to pester me again. Never!"

"We promise! We promise!"

Aunt Misery released them from her pear tree. The rascals scrambled off, never to pester her again.

She lived peacefully for many years. One day, though, another traveler knocked on her door. His face was hidden in the folds of his long, dark hood. Aunt Misery had a bad feeling about him. Her hunch was right. He said, "I am Death. Come with me."

Aunt Misery stayed calm, but her mind was thinking. "I'll come right away. But first let me get a jug of cool water and a basket of pears for our journey."

"Be quick about it," said Death. "I have many visits today."

Aunt Misery brought out a jug of water and an empty basket. "Would you be so kind as to help me? I can't climb my tree like I used to. Could you just get on that first branch and hand down some pears?"

"All right, if it will make you come any faster," said Death. Grumbling and complaining, he climbed into the pear tree, picked some fruit, and threw it down to Aunt Misery. "Let's be on our way," he called out. When he tried to climb down, he was struck. The harder he struggled, the harder he stuck. "Old woman, you let me down right now or you will be sorry."

"Not as sorry as you will be for messing with Aunt Misery." She went into her hut and shut the door.

Death stayed stuck, like a fly in a web. People came from miles around just to see him sitting up in that tree. What a grand sight to see.

Time passed and no one died. It would be nice to report that no one got older either, but that's not what happened. Everyone got older. At first, an endless life seemed like a blessing. Then it seemed like a curse. Some complained they were tired; some complained they were sick. People began to demand that Aunt Misery let Death climb down from the pear tree, so he could do his job.

Aunt Misery liked her long life; she was still fit and spry. But she saw the world was getting crowded and food was scant to feed all those mouths. Finally, she made an offer. "Death, I'll let you climb down from my tree, so you can go about your business. But you must never pester me again. Never!"

Death nodded. "If you let me go, you have seen the last of me."

Aunt Misery and Death kept their bargain. She freed him; he spared her. That is why, dear amigos, from that day to this—Misery remains in the world.

Sadie and Bessie Delany

1889–1999 and 1891–1995

The Delany Sisters were first introduced to the world in 1991 when Amy Hill Hearth wrote an article for the *New York Times.* The story of Bessie and Sadie Delany, both over one hundred years old, created so much interest that the editors of Kodansha America, Inc. asked the women to write their memoirs. For eighteen months, Hearth sat in the sisters' kitchen and garden in Mount Vernon, New York, and recorded their oral histories. Hearth said, "I let the sisters speak for themselves."[1]

In *Having Our Say: The Delany Sisters' First 100 Years,* they recall their childhood as two of ten children. Their father, Henry Beard Delany, born a slave on a Georgia plantation, was freed upon Emancipation. Their parents met while students at Saint Augustine's School in Raleigh, North Carolina. "Papa" became vice principal and "Mama" the matron. All ten children were raised on the Saint Augustine campus.

When grown, nine of the Delany children, including Sadie and Bessie, joined the mass movement to the northern cities away from the Jim Crow laws of the South. They moved to Harlem just before the Roaring '20s. Sadie earned her master's degree from Columbia University and became New York City's first black high school teacher of home economics. Bessie received her degree in dentistry from Columbia University, became one of only two licensed black female dentists, and opened her own practice.

Having Our Say was on the New York Times Bestseller List for twenty-eight weeks and sold 350,000 copies in hardcover and 500,000 copies in paperback. The book was translated into Japanese, Spanish, German, and Italian—"Not bad for two old inky-dinks over one hundred years old!" joked Bessie.[2] The book was adapted into a play, which ran in New York City in 1995 and in 1996 at the Kennedy Center's Eisenhower Theater as part of a fifty-city tour.

Letters poured in to the sisters, often with questions on how to live a long life. In lieu of writing a personal reply to each letter, Bessie and Sadie did a follow-up book with Amy Hill Hearth. In *The Delany Sisters' Book of Everyday Wisdom*, they shared their secrets of long life. They said, "We're as old as Moses, so maybe we have learned a few things along the way, and we'd like to pass them on."[3] Here are three of their many suggestions:

EXERCISE DAILY

Sadie said, "We get up with the sun, and the first thing we do is exercise. God gave you only one body, so you better be nice to it. Exercise, because if you don't, by the time you're our age, you'll be pushing up daisies."[4]

More than forty years before, she noticed that her "Mama" was "starting to shrink up and get bent down."[5] Sadie began exercising with her. When Bessie turned eighty, she wanted to look as good as Sadie, so they both followed a yoga program on television. After their first book was published, the sisters even demonstrated yoga on a television show with Charles Kuralt.

EAT VEGETABLES

The sisters believed in eating vegetables, mostly those home-grown by Bessie. The habit started in childhood. The farm on the St. Augustine campus provided food for the staff and students. The children worked in the fields to earn a little money.

During World War II, their apartment in Harlem had no room for a garden. The sisters went to their cousin's in the Bronx to raise a Victory Garden.[6] After the war, they bought a little cottage next to their Victory Garden.

When a housing project was built across the street from the Delanys', the project children stole fruit from their neighbor's trees. But these children never bothered the sisters. Sadie explained:

We were nicer to the children. We went out and said to them, "The fruit on our peach trees isn't ripe yet, so please leave it alone. But when it's ripe, you come by and we'll share it with you." And we did. And those children never harmed us, or our trees or anything we owned.[7]

Finally, in 1957, the sisters moved to a house in Mount Vernon; Bessie continued her gardening. In the summer, they picked and cooked whatever was ripe for dinner. Bessie said, "We just know those vegetables keep us healthy. We make it a point to eat seven different vegetables every day."[8] Sadie included her recipe for Seven Vegetable Casserole in *Everyday Wisdom.*

STAY SINGLE

Sadie said, "When people ask me how we've lived past 100, I say, 'Honey, we never married; we never had husbands to worry us to death.'"[9]

Postscript: On September 25, 1995, at the age of 104, Bessie died at home with Sadie nearby. Sadie continued to live in their house and wrote a book in tribute to her younger sister, On My Own: Reflections on Life Without Bessie. *She began the book, "I sure miss you, Old Gal." On January 26, 1999, at the age of 109, Sadie died in her sleep at her Mount Vernon home.*

NOTES

INTRODUCTION

1.   Kathleen Noble, *The Sound of the Silver Horn: Reclaiming the Heroism in Contemporary Women's Lives* (New York: Fawcett Columbine, 1994), 240.

2.   Ellen Sue Stern, *In My Prime: Meditations for Women in Midlife* (New York: Dell Publishing, 1995), month four, day sixteen.

ROSES

1.   Welleran Poltarnees, *Women and Flowers* (Hong Kong: Blue Lantern Books, 1993), 18.

2.   Elaine Partnow, *The New Quotable Woman* (New York: Meridian, 1993), 343.

BREAD AND ROSES

Saint Elizabeth of Hungary lived from 1207 to 1231. Her husband, Ludwig, died of the plague on a crusade. His brothers accused Elizabeth of mismanaging the estate because of her charities and forced her and her children to leave. She joined the Franciscan order. Known as "the Patroness of the Poor," she cared for the sick, poor, and aged until her death; she was canonized in 1235. See John J. Delaney, *Dictionary of Saints* (New York: Doubleday and Company, 1980), 194–195.

I like to think the flowers that appeared in Elizabeth's basket were wild roses and were used in a tea for her husband. Folklore says tea from the petals of a wild rose will change the very nature of a malefactor. See Valerie Worth, *Crone's Book of Charms and Spells* (St. Paul, MN: Llewellyn Publications, 1998), 18.

Liz Warren, a Phoenix storyteller who loves this legend, was inspired to write this haiku:

> *Saint Elizabeth*
> *shower us with rose petals.*
> *No more bread, she says.*

Sources include:

Katharine M. Beals, *Flower Lore and Legend* (New York: Henry Holt and Company, 1917).

Hugh Francis Blunt, "St. Elizabeth of Hungary," in *Great Wives and Mothers* (New York: Devin-Adair Company, 1917).

M.A. Jagendorf, "The Miracle of the Rose," in *The Priceless Cats and Other Italian Folk Stories* (New York: Vanguard Press, 1956).

Charles Skinner, *Myths and Legends of Flowers Trees, Fruits, and Plants* (Philadelphia. J.D. Lippincott Company, 1911).

MARGARET OLIVIA SLOCUM SAGE

1. Time-Life Books, "The Sage of Wall Street," in *Odd and Eccentric People* (Alexandria, VA: Time-Life Books, 1920), 42.

2. Paul Sarnoff, *Russell Sage: The Money King* (New York: Ivan Obolensky, 1965), 321.

3. Ibid., 319, 327.

4. *Dictionary of American Biography*, s.v. "Margaret Olivia Slocum Sage."

5. Time-Life Books, "The Sage of Wall Street," 42.

THE CUNNING OF FINN'S WIFE

Two of the most celebrated Irish heroes, Finn mac Cumhaill and Cu Chulainn, were warriors with magical powers. Cu Chulainn was the central figure in the *Ulster Cycle* of tales. Finn was the main character in the *Fennian Cycle* of tales. Finn, born of a divine father, had the gift of prophecy, which he obtained when he caught the salmon of Linn Feic. Finn cooked—but was forbidden to eat—the salmon which would bestow all knowledge on the person who ate it. Finn burned his thumb on the cooking salmon, popped it into his mouth, and discovered he possessed all knowledge. Under the influence of Christianity, these pagan heroes were reduced to folk heroes who appear in fireside tales. See Anne Ross, "Finn" in *Man, Myth and Magic: The Illustrated Encyclopedia of Mythology, Religion and the Unknown,* ed. Richard Cavendish (New York: Marshall Cavendish, 1985), 964–967.

Sources include:

Eunice Fuller, "The Cunning of Fin's Wife," in *The Book of Friendly Giants* (New York: Century Company, 1914).

Joseph Jacobs, "A Legend of Knockmany," in *Celtic Folk and Fairy Tales* (New York: G.P. Putnam's Sons, n.d.).

William Butler Yeats, "A Legend of Knockmany," in *Irish Folk Stories and Fairy Tales* (New York: Grosset and Dunlap, 1974).

EDITH BOLLING WILSON

1. Edith Wilson, *My Memoirs* (New York: Bobbs-Merrill, 1938), 86.

2. Ibid., 286.

3. Ibid., 289.

4. Ibid.

5. Arthur S. Link, "Wilson, Edith Bolling Galt," in *Notable American Women: The Modern Period* (Cambridge: Harvard University Press, Belknap Press, 1980), 740.

6. Wilson, *My Memoirs*, 289.

7. James Cross Giblin, *Edith Wilson: The Woman Who Ran the United States* (New York: Viking, 1992), 40–41.

DEMETER AND PERSEPHONE

One of the earliest cults of Demeter was centered in Mycenae in the thirteenth century B.C. The cult spread throughout Greece; Eleusis was the center of the religion that survived for about two thousand years. See Barbara G. Walker, "Demeter," in *The Woman's Encyclopedia of Myths and Secrets* (New York: Harper and Row, 1983), 218–221.

In his poem, *Hymn to Demeter,* Homer says that before Demeter returned to Olympus, she taught the Eleusinian king and court the science of cultivation and agriculture. She also initiated them into her Mysteries, the rites they were to practice at her temple. See Sir James George Frazier, "Demeter and Persephone," in *The Golden Bough: A Study in Magic and Religion,* vol. 1, abridged ed. (New York: Macmillan Company, 1951), 457–459.

The Eleusinian Mysteries were the most sacred of the ritual celebrations of ancient Greece. Each fall, thousands of worshippers gathered in Athens to make the holy pilgrimage to Eleusis. They walked the Sacred Road, approximately fourteen miles, between the two cities to participate in the secret rites.

When they arrived at Eleusis, the pilgrims danced all night at the well where Demeter mourned for Persephone. Then they passed through the gates into the temple that held up to three thousand people. Because the participants pledged not to reveal what happened in the inner sanctum, the exact nature of the Mysteries is unknown. To violate that oath of secrecy was a capital offense. See Antonia Fraser, "Demeter and Persephone," in *Heroes and Heroines* (New York: A&W Publishers, 1980), 24–26.

The Demeter rituals came to an end in the fourth century with the invasion of the Goths. Little remains of the great Sanctuary at Eleusis. As the invaders imposed their patriarchal religion on the conquered peoples, the male deities took the prominent place and the female goddesses faded into the background. Later, the Hebrew and Christian religions completed the dethroning of Demeter. See Jean Shinoda Bolen, M.D., *Goddesses in Everywoman: A New Psychology of Women* (New York: Harper and Row, Harper Colophon Books, 1984), 20–21.

SOURCES INCLUDE:

Homer, *The Homeric Hymns,* trans. Thelma Sargent (New York: Norton, 1973).

Ann Pilling, "Persephone," in *Realms of Gold: Myths and Legends From Around the World* (New York: Kingfisher Books, 1993).

Penelope Proddow, *Demeter and Persephone* (New York: Doubleday and Company, 1972).

ELIZABETH MORGAN

1. Elizabeth Morgan, M.D,. *Custody: A True Story* (Boston: Little, Brown and Company, 1986), 81.

2. Ibid., 250.

3. Jon Elson, "A Hard Case of Contempt," *Time*, 18 September 1989, 66.

4. Jonathan Groner, *Hilary's Trial: The Elizabeth Morgan Case* (New York: Simon & Schuster, American Lawyer Books, 1991), 244.

5. Ibid., 255–256, 265–266.

6. Ibid., 276.

7. Nora Underwood, "A Child's Odyssey: Police Find a Missing Girl in New Zealand," *McLean's*, 12 March 1990, 56–57.

8. Bill Miller, "Congress Votes to Let Morgan Return," *Washington Post*, 19 September 1996, final ed., A1.

9. "Foretich Sues Over 'Morgan Law'," *Washington Post*, 2 May 1997, B3.

10. Ibid.

SPIDER BRINGS THE FIRE

Like Spider, who brought fire, the Cherokee Rose also brought comfort to the Cherokee. According to the Legend of the Cherokee Rose, during the forced march out of their ancestral lands the mothers grieved so hard that the people prayed for a symbol to lift their spirits and give them strength to care for the children. From that day forward, wherever a mother's tear fell to the ground, a rose sprang up. The rose has white petals, for the mothers' tears, and a gold center, for the gold taken from the Cherokee lands. To this day, the Cherokee Rose blooms along the route. It is now the official flower of the State of Georgia. No better symbol exists of the pain and suffering of the "Trail Where They Cried" than the Cherokee Rose.

SOURCES INCLUDE:

I heard the beautiful Gayle Ross tell a version of this story in 1995 at the International Storytelling Festival in Wales. She is a Texan, a direct descendant of Cherokee chief John Ross, and the author of *How Rabbit Tricked Otter and Other Cherokee Trickster Stories* (New York: HarperCollins, 1994).

Paula Gunn Allen, "A Hot Time," in *Grandmothers of the Light: A Medicine Woman's Sourcebook* (Boston: Beacon Press, 1991).

Katharine Berry Judson, "The First Fire," in *Myths and Legends of the Great Plains*, (Chicago: A.C. McClurg and Company, 1913).

George F. Scheer, "The First Fire," in *Cherokee Animal Tales* (New York: Holiday House, 1968).

WILMA PEARL MANKILLER

1. "Wilma Mankiller," in *Biography Today*, ed. Laurie Lanzen Harris (Detroit: Omnigraphic, Inc., 1994), 216.

2. Della A. Yannuzzi, *Wilma Mankiller: Leader of the Cherokee Nation* (Hillside, NJ: Enslow Publisher, 1994), 5.

3. Ibid., 6–8.

4. Wilma Mankiller and Michael Wallis, *Mankiller: A Chief and Her People* (New York: St. Martin's Press, 1993). 233–235.

5. "Wilma Mankiller," in *Biography Today*, 222.

6. "Cherokee Losing Chief Who Revitalized Tribe," *New York Times*, 6 April 1994, A9(N), A16(L).

THE FAIRIES' MIDWIFE

SOURCES INCLUDE:

Katharine M. Briggs, "Fairy Ointment," in *An Encyclopedia of Fairies* (New York: Pantheon Books, 1976).

Dov Noy, "The Reward of a Midwife," in *Folktales of Israel* (Chicago: University of Chicago Press).

Josepha Sherman, "The Demon's Midwife," in *Jewish-American Folklore* (Little Rock: August House, 1992).

Enys Tregarthen, "The Nurse Who Broke Her Promise," in *Piskey Folk: A Book of Cornish Legends* (New York: John Day Company, 1940).

ONNIE LEE LOGAN

1. Deborah Sullivan and Rose Weitz, *Labor Pains* (New Haven: Yale University Press, 1988), 1.

2. Molly Ladd-Taylor, "Midwifery," in *The Reader's Companion to U.S. Women's History*, ed. Wilma Mankiller, Gwendolyn Mink, Marysa Navarro, Barbara Smith, and Gloria Steinem (New York: Houghton Mifflin Company, 1998), 369.

3. Onnie Lee Logan as told to Katherine Clark, *Motherwit* (New York: E.P. Dutton, 1989), 64.

4. Ibid., 87.

5. Ibid., 89.

6. Ibid., 140.

7. Ibid., 130.

8. Ibid., 176.

9. Marian Wright Edelman, "Spiritual Salt," *New York Times Magazine*, 31 December 1995, 38.

10. Michael Lewis, "Driving Miss Onnie," *New Republic*, 16 August 1993, 11–12.

11. Logan, *Motherwit*, 177.

GODMOTHER DEATH

SOURCES INCLUDE:

Parker Fillmore, "The Candles of Life," in *The Shoemaker's Apron* (New York: Harcourt, Brace and Company, 1920).

Jose Griego y Maestas and Rudolfo A. Anaya, "Dona Sebastiana," in *Cuentos: Tales from the Hispanic Southwest* (Santa Fe: Museum of New Mexico Press, 1980).

John O. West, "Dona Sebastiana," in *Mexican-American Folklore* (Little Rock: August House, 1988).

Riley Aiken, "La Madrina Muerte," in *Puro Mexicano,* ed. Frank J. Dobie (Dallas: Southern University Press, 1980).

TERESA URREA

1. William Curry Holden, *Teresita* (Owings Mill, MD: Stemmer House, 1978), 54.

2. Diane Telgen and Jim Kamp, "Teresa Urrea," in *Notable Hispanic American Women* (Detroit: Gale Research, 1993), 405.

3. Holden, *Teresita,* 56.

4. Sam Negri, "Teresita, The Saint of Cabora," *Arizona Highways,* 14 March 1994, 13–14.

BERURIAH'S JEWELS

The Talmud forbids announcing bad news clearly and bluntly. To announce death in a roundabout way is traditional. Hanging a piece of linen in front of the door or pouring out all the water in the house are signals to the neighbors of a death. See Dr. Angelo S. Rappoport, *The Folklore of the Jews* (London: Soncino Press, 1937), 103.

SOURCES INCLUDE:

Nathan Ausubel, "The Value of a Good Wife," in *The Treasury of Jewish Folklore* (New York: Crown Publishers, 1975). From the Talmud, translated by Samuel T. Coleridge, in *Hebrew Tales,* by Hyman Hurwitz (London: Morrison and Watt, 1826).

Judith Ish-Kishor, "Beruriah and the Treasure," in *Tales from the Wise Men of Israel* (New York: J.B. Lippincott Company, 1962).

ROSE FITZGERALD KENNEDY

1. Rose Fitzgerald Kennedy, *Times to Remember* (New York: Doubleday and Company, 1974), 442.

2. Ibid., 445.

3. Ibid., 475.

4. Ibid., 476.

5. Ibid., 477.

6. Ibid.

7. Ibid., 482.

8. Mark Goodman, "The Last Matriarch," *People Weekly,* 6 February 1995, 36–39.

SAINT BRIGID'S CLOAK

Folklore contains various spellings of the goddess/saint: Bridget, Brigit, Brigid. In Ireland, the goddess Brigid became Saint Brigid, or Bride. Belief in the goddess Brigid was brought to the island by the Gaelic Celts, perhaps between the fifth century B.C. and the first century A.D. She was the divinity of fire, agriculture, animal husbandry, healing, smithcraft, and poetry. Her day was

February 1, the Feast of Imbolc, one of the four Celtic seasonal festivals. This event marked the first day of spring and the beginning of plowing and sowing. Her shrine at Kildare was attended by nineteen priestesses who kept a sacred fire ever burning. See Barbara G. Walker, "Saint Brigit," in *The Woman's Encyclopedia of Myths and Secrets* (New York: Harper and Row, 1983), 116–118.

With the arrival of Christianity, the early church wanted to undermine the remnants of paganism by converting new populations, yet unsettle the local practices as little as possible. This policy was reflected in a letter in which Pope Gregory the Great directed Saint Augustine to destroy idols but turn the pagan temples into churches, so that local people would have a familiar worship place for the new faith. Pagan goddesses that could not be obliterated were to be converted into saints. See Pamela Berger, *The Goddess Obscured: Transformation of the Grain Goddess to Saint* (Boston: Beacon Press, 1986), 50.

Unable to eradicate the cult of Brigid, around 525 A.D., the Catholic church claimed that she was a saint, founder, and abbess of a convent at Kildare. There are many accounts of Saint Brigid's birth and upbringing; some reports say she was born to a pagan father, the Arch-Druid to the High King of Tara, but was converted to Christianity by Saint Patrick. Tradition says that she is buried in one grave with Saint Patrick and Saint Columba. See E. Lucia Turnbull, "Little Miracle," in *Legends of the Saints* (New York: J.B. Lippincott Company, 1981), 29, 108–109.

In spite of her transformation, the links between goddess and saint remained. It is reported that the Christian nuns continued to keep Brigid's fire ablaze until the Normans extinguished it in the twelfth century. Her feast day remained February 1. On Imbolc/Saint Brigid's Day, straw from the previous harvest was woven into shapes. During the age of the goddess, these straw shapes, symbols of the sun, were used to protect cattle. From the fifth century until now, the very same shapes are called Saint Brigid's Cross and used to protect houses. Whether pagan or Christian, Brigid was revered for her magical or miraculous acts of kindness and charity. See Daragh Smyth, *A Guide to Irish Mythology* (Dublin: Irish Academic Press, 1996), 26.

Sources include:

Marie Heaney, "Saint Brigid," in *Over Nine Waves* (Boston: Faber and Faber, 1994).

Patrick Kennedy, "St. Brigid's Cloak," in *Great Folk Tales of Ireland,* ed. Mary McGarry (London: Frederick Muller, 1972).

E. Lucia Turnbull, "The Cloak of St. Bridget," in *Legends of the Saints* (New York: J.B. Lippincott Company, 1981).

SAINT FRANCIS XAVIER CABRINI

1. Anne Gordon, *A Book of Saints* (New York: Bantam Books, 1994), 131.
2. Pietro Di Donanto, *Immigrant Saint: The Life of Mother Cabrini* (New York: St. Martin's Press, 1990), 214–216.

MOST HONORED

This brief folktale was the inspiration for my version:

"The Greatest Person…," in *The Sower's Seeds: One Hundred Inspiring Stories for Preaching, Teaching and Public Speaking,* ed. Brian Cavanaugh (New York: Paulist Press, 1990).

MARY McLEOD BETHUNE

1. Patricia C. McKissack, *Mary McLeod Bethune: A Great American Educator* (Chicago: Childrens Press, 1985), 41.

2. Lynn Sherr and Jurate Kazickas, *Susan B. Anthony Slept Here: A Guide to American Women's Landmarks* (New York: Random House, 1994), 97.

3. McKissack, *Mary McLeod Bethune,* 86–87.

4. Sherr and Kazickas, *Susan B. Anthony Slept Here,* 90–91.

ELISABETH, MOTHER OF JOHN THE BAPTIST

With Christianity, the rose became associated with the Virgin Mary. One belief, which dates to the second century, holds that when Mary's tomb was opened to show Thomas that her body had ascended to heaven, it was filled with roses and lillies.

During the twelfth century, St. Dominic conceived the idea of the rosary while holding a garland of red and white roses. The Rosary is called "Roses of Prayer for the Queen of Heaven."

Our Lady of Guadalupe is a popular legend in Mexico. In December 1531, the Virgin Mary appeared to a poor Indian, Juan Diego. She asked him to convey her request to the bishop of Mexico that a church be built in her honor on the hill at Tepeyac. As a sign of her presence, she caused a variety of roses to bloom out of season on the barren hillside. Juan Diego filled his *tilma* with the roses and carried them to the church palace. When he spread the roses before the bishop, his tilma was marked with the life-sized image of the Virgin. The Church of Our Lady of Guadalupe was built on the hillside and the tilma adorned the altar.

SOURCE of Biblical passage: Luke 1:5–80. Authorized King James Version.

ARLETTE SCHWEITZER

1. J. Madeleine Nash, "All in the Family," *Time,* 19 August 1991, 58.

2. Ibid.

3. Annie Griffiths Belt and Claudia Glenn Dowling, "Miraculous Babies," *Life,* December 1993, 75–82.

4. Nash, "All in the Family," 58.

5. Arlette Schweitzer, "My Children, My Grandchildren," *Ladies Home Journal,* February 1992, 125–131.

6 "Now They Are One," *People Weekly,* 26 October 1992, 165.

THE LION'S WHISKERS

SOURCES INCLUDE:

Russell Davis and Brent Ashabranner, "The Lion's Whiskers," in *The*

Lion's Whiskers: Tales of High Africa (Boston: Little, Brown and Company, 1959).

Nancy Raines Day, *The Lion's Whiskers: An Ethiopian Folktale* (New York: Scholastic, 1995).

Edna Mason Kaula, "The Tiger's Whiskers," in *African Village Folktales* (New York: World, 1968).

SARAH BUSH JOHNSTON LINCOLN

Floribunda roses bear clusters of flowers on a single stem; several flowers open at one time. Stepmothers who gather their stepchildren into families are like floribunda roses, because the cluster is more significant than an individual blossom. One unique floribunda is the "Love" rose, whose red petals have white undersides.

1. Michael Burlingame, *The Inner World of Abraham Lincoln* (Chicago: University of Illinois, 1994), 95.

2. Carl Sandburg, *Abraham Lincoln: The Prairie Years and the War Years,* one-volume edition (New York: Harcourt, Brace and World, 1949), 12.

3. Louis A. Warren, *Lincoln's Youth: Indiana Years, Seven to Twenty-one, 1816–1830* (New York: Appleton, Century, Crofts, 1959), 54.

4. William H. Herndon and Jess W. Weik, *Herndon's Life of Lincoln* (New York: World, 1930), 27.

5. Warren, *Lincoln's Youth,* 65.

6. Laura C. Holloway, *The Mothers* (Philadelphia: Calypso Publishing Company, 1887), 125.

7. Warren, *Lincoln's Youth,* 66.

8. Donna Smith, *Stepmothering* (New York: St. Martin's Press, 1990), 43.

9. Herndon, *Life of Lincoln,* 30.

THE LADY AND THE UNJUST JUDGE

SOURCES INCLUDE:

Milton Rugoff, "The Lady and the Unjust Judge," in *A Harvest of World Folk Tales* (New York: Viking Press, 1949). Retold from Allan Ramay and Francis McCullagh, *Tales from Turkey* (London: Simpkin, Marshall, Hamilton, Kent and Company, 1914).

John Faulkner, *Judge Not!* (Chicago: Albert Whitman, 1968).

BELVA ANN LOCKWOOD

1. Marian Calabro, "Belva Lockwood," in *Great Courtroom Lawyers: Fighting the Cases That Made History* (New York: FactsOnFile, 1996), 5.

2. Madeleine B. Stern, "Belva Ann Lockwood," in *We the Women* (Lincoln: University of Nebraska Press, 1962), 231.

3. Phyllis Raybin Emert, "Belva Lockwood," in *Top Lawyers and their Famous Cases* (Minneapolis: Oliver Press, 1996), 72.

4. Mary Virginia Fox, *Lady for the Defense: A Biography of Belva Lockwood* (New York: Harcourt Brace Jovanovich, 1975), 147.

5. Stern, "Belva Ann Lockwood," 231.

HOLDING UP THE SKY

SOURCES INCLUDE:

Isabelle C. Chang, "The World's Work," in *Tales from Old China* (New York: Random House, 1969).

Elizabeth Layton, quoted in "A Hidden Talent" by Michael Ryan, *Parade Magazine,* 28 May 1989.

Margaret Read MacDonald, "Holding Up the Sky," in *Peace Tales: World Folktales to Talk About* (Hamden, CT: Linnet Books, 1992).

JUSTINE MERRITT

A fitting rose for Justine Merritt would be the Peace rose, a yellow hybid tea rose, developed in France in 1945. It was smuggled out of Paris in the last U.S. diplomatic pouch to leave before the Nazi occupation. After World War II ended, the rose was named to celebrate peace and became one of the most beloved roses of all time.

1. *The Ribbon: A Celebration of Life,* ed. Lark Books Staff and Marianne Philbin (Asheville, NC: Lark Books, 1985), 14.

2. David Grogan, "A Pentagon Ribbon for Peace," in *People Weekly, 8* July 1985, 20–23.

3. Justine Merritt, introduction to *The Ribbon: A Celebration of Life,* ed. Lark Books Staff and Marianne Philbin (Asheville, NC: Lark Books, 1985), 12.

4. Grogan, "A Pentagon Ribbon for Peace," 20.

5. Linda Pershing, "Peace Work out of Piecework: Feminist Needlework Metaphors and The Ribbon around the Pentagon," in *Feminine Theory and the Study of Folklore,* ed. Susan Tower Hollis, Linda Pershing, and M. Jane Young (Chicago: University of Illinois Press, 1993), 337.

6. Ibid., 332, 351.

7. Ibid., 351.

8. Ibid., 331–332, 339.

9. Merritt, introduction to *The Ribbon,* 13.

THE CRUEL WAR IS RAGING

SOURCE: Irwin Silber and Fred Silber, ed., *Folksinger's Wordbook* (New York: Oak Publications, 1973), 272.

MARGARET COCHRAN CORBIN

Her story has sometimes been confused with that of Mary Hays McCauley, another Revolutionary war hero who fought by her husband's side. Both women have been called "Molly Pitcher," which was a nickname for women who carried water to troops during battle.

1. Jessica Amanda Salmonson, *The Encyclopedia of Amazons* (New York: Paragon House, 1991), 48, 64.

2. J. Clement, "Margaret Corbin," in *Noble Deeds of American Women* (Boston: Lee and Sheppard, 1875), 27.

3. Lynn Sherr and Jurate Kazickas, *Susan B. Anthony Slept Here: A Guide to American Women's Landmarks* (New York: Random House, 1994), 324, 336.

THE WISE OLD WOMAN

The wise old woman is like the rose hip from a dog rose because her wisdom holds the seeds for future generations. The dog rose remains useful even after its petals have fallen. The rose head forms a large, bright red rose hip, a seeded fruit, which has been a food source since prehistoric times. Its nutritious fruit is used to make jams, jellies, and an old German soup, *Hagebutten.* Steeped for tea, the rose hip is sweet, tangy, and full of vitamin C and flavonoids. During World War II, hips were gathered from the English hedgerows and made into syrup for the children.

SOURCES INCLUDE:

Linda Gan, "Taro and his Grandmother," in *A Treasury of Asian Tales* (San Diego: Dominie Press, 1992).

Babette Deutsch, "Grandfather's Advice," in *Tales of Faraway Folk* (New York: Harper and Brothers, 1952).

Fanny Hagin Mayer, "The Mountain Where Old Women Were Abandoned," in *Ancient Tales in Modern Japan* (Bloomington: Indiana University Press, 1984).

James Riordan, "The Golden Vase," in *Tales from Tartary: Russian Tales,* bk. 2 (New York: Viking Press, 1978).

Velma Wallis, *Two Old Women* (Fairbanks: Epicenter Press, 1993).

Yoshiko Uchida, *The Wise Old Woman* (New York: Macmillan, Margaret K. McElderry Books, 1994).

MAGGIE KUHN

1. Lynn Gilbert and Gaylen Moore, *Particular Passions: Talks with Women Who Have Shaped Our Times* (New York: Clarkson N. Potter, 1981), 103.

2. Robert McG. Thomas Jr., "Maggie Kuhn, 89, the founder of the Gray Panthers, is dead" (Obituary), *New York Times,* 23 April 1995, 22(N) 47(L).

3. Jane Seskin, *More Than Mere Survival: Conversations with Women Over 65* (New York: Newsweek Books, 1980), 129.

4. Lois Decker O'Neill, *The Women's Book of World Records and Achievements* (Garden City: Doubleday, Anchor Press, 1979), 722.

5. Maggie Kuhn with Christa Long and Laura Quinn, *No Stone Unturned: The Life and Times of Maggie Kuhn* (New York: Ballantine Books, 1991), 143.

6. Seskin, *More Than Mere Survival,* 133.

7. *Gray Panthers' NETWORK News,* Spring 1995, 16–17.

NOT ROSES

1. Ai Ja Lee, quoted in *What We Know So Far: Wisdom Among Women,* ed. Beth Benatovich (Thorndike, ME: G.K. Hall and Company, 1995), 207. This is a prose quote that I arranged into poetic form.

2. Carolyn G. Heilbrun, *Writing a Woman's Life* (New York: Ballantine, 1989), 131.

LILITH

The legend of Lilith is not in the Bible. Versions are found in the *Midrash* and post-biblical rabbinic writings. The Lilith legend was possibly an attempt to reconcile seeming contradictions between the creation in Genesis 1 and 2. See Nathan Ausubel, ed., *A Treasury of Jewish Folklore* (New York: Crown Publishers, 1975), 446, 593.

One interpretation of Genesis 1:27 is that man and woman were created simultaneously:

> So God created man in His Image, in the Image of God created he him; male and female created he them.

By contrast, in Genesis 2:18, 21, 22, man was created first:

> And the Lord God said, It is not good that the man should be alone; I will make him an help meet for him. And the LORD God caused a deep sleep to fall upon Adam, and he slept: and he took one of his ribs, and closed up the flesh instead hereof; And the rib, which the Lord God had taken from man, made he a woman, and brought her unto the man.

These versions are two different creation stories. Genesis 1 derives from a Sumerian story, while Genesis 2 is a later creation of the Hebrew priesthood. However, the rabbis, who wrote interpretations and commentaries of the Bible and took the scriptures as truth, demanded an explanation that reconciled both stories. The rabbis decided the first passage referred to the creation of Lilith, Adam's first wife. See Howard Schwartz, *Lilith's Cave: Jewish Tales of the Supernatural* (New York: Harper and Row, 1988), 5.

Contemporary feminists claim that Judaism demonized Lilith as a baby killer and whore. Religion professor Judith Plaskow says the Jewish patriarchy gave Lilith a "lousy reputation" as the "ultimate uppity woman." See Lynn Gottlieb, *She Who Dwells Within: A Feminist Vision of a Renewed Judaism* (San Francisco: Harper, 1995), 54–55. Writer Lilly Rivlin deplores the "deformed and evil archetype" that assails the female qualities of sensuality, passion, and independence. See Martha Weigle, *Spiders and Spinsters: Women and Mythology* (Albuquerque: University of New Mexico, 1982), 255.

To many feminists, Lilith is an icon because she represents the instinctually free spirit of the feminine and the first woman to defy male domination. The World Wide Web has several sites featuring Lilith, including "The Lilith Shrine." *LILITH* is the name of "The Independent Jewish Women's Magazine." The magazine, published since 1994, "helps Jewish women rediscover and rework traditions, combat sterotypes, explore new paths to Jewish learning and celebration, and work for inclusive social and ritual change."

The myriad of Lilith legends are primarily Middle Eastern; there is, however, a Norwegian variant, "The Origin of the Huldre Folk." That version says that God put Lilith and her children by Adam out of Eden, because it was not good for a woman to be equal. Those children became the *huldre*, the tall beautiful elfin folk; they are without sin because they left the Garden before the Fall.

SOURCES INCLUDE:

Nathan Ausubel, "Demon Tales," in *A Treasury of Jewish Folklore* (New York: Crown Publishers, 1975).

J.E. Hanauer, "Our Father Adam," in *Folklore of the Holy Land* (London: Sheldon Press, 1935).

Barbara Black Koltuv, *The Book of Lilith* (York Beach, ME: Nicolas-Hays, 1986).

Robert Graves and Raphael Patai, *Hebrew Myths: The Book of Genesis* (New York: Greenwich Books, 1983).

MAE WEST

1. Mae West, *Goodness Had Nothing to Do with It* (Englewood Cliffs, NJ: Prentice-Hall, 1959), 29.

2. Ibid., 96–100.

3. Marybeth Hamilton, *When I'm Bad, I'm Better: Mae West, Sex, and American Entertainment* (New York: HarperCollins 1995), 187.

4. George Ells and Stanley Musgrove, *Mae West* (New York: William Morrow and Company, 1982), 167–185

5. West, *Goodness,* 195.

BOADICEA: WARRIOR QUEEN

There are three primary sources for the history of Boadicea. Two were written by Tacitus, the first of which was reported about 98 A.D. in *Agricola,* the biography of his father-in-law, who was in Britain at the time of the rebellion. The second account, in his *Annals of Imperial Rome,* was written fifteen to twenty years later. The third source comes from Cassius Dio, who was born a hundred years after the events. Though archaeological discoveries have verified that the battles took place, it cannot be determined how much of the recorded histories are myth. Perhaps Tacitus exaggerated the casualties for dramatic effect. Perhaps Dio's descriptions of Boadicea and her speech were drawn from popular assumptions about the Celts.

1. From a version of Dio's account, see Antonia Fraser, "Iceni: The Powerful Tribe," in *The Warrior Queens* (New York: Random House, Vintage Books, 1990), 55–56.

2. Tacitus, *Annals,* bk. 14, chap. 31. I found this adaptation of Arthur Murphy's translation (*Works of Tacitus,* 1794) on the *Athena Review* website, [http://www.athenapub.com/britsite/tacitus1.htm].

3. Ibid., chap. 30.

4. As reported by the Roman historian, Dio, see Maurice Saxby, "Boadicea: Queen of the Iceni," in *The Great Deeds of Heroic Women* (New York: Peter Bedrick Books, 1990), 100.

5. Fraser, *Warrior Queens,* 70–71.

6. Tacitus, *Annals,* chap. 32.

7. Tacitus, *Annals,* chap. 33.

8. Saxby, "Boadicea"103.

9. Tacitus, *Annals,* chap. 37.

LOZEN: APACHE WARRIOR

Lozen could be represented by the lotebush. In the years she was in flight from the cavalry, perhaps she used lotebush, also called condalia. The desert shrub, known for its little clusters of creamy flowers, grows in the desert Southwest. The Apache boiled its fresh root to make a shampoo. They also made a tea from its dried root to bathe the backs and flanks of injured horses.

1. Susan Haze Hammond, "Lozen: Apache Warrior, Holy Woman, and a Shield to Her People," *Arizona Highways,* February 1996, 10.

2. Zachary Kent, *The Story of Geronimo* (Chicago: Children's Press, 1989), 12–14.

3. Time-Life Books, "Geronimo and the White Eyes," in *Defiant Chiefs* (Alexandria, VA: Time-Life Books, 1997), 163.

4. Henrietta Stockel, *Women of the Apache Nation: Voices of Truth* (Reno: University of Nevada Press, 1991), 47.

5. Eve Ball, *In the Days of Victorio: Recollections of a Warm Spring Apache* (Tucson: University of Arizona Press, 1970), 15.

6. Hammond, "Lozen: Apache Warrior," 13.

7. Kent, *Geronimo,* 5, 24.

8. Time-Life, *Great Chiefs,* 43.

THE REALLY DANGEROUS POST

SOURCES INCLUDE:

Kemp P. Battle, "A Patient Wife," in *Great American Folklore: Legends, Tales, Ballads, and Superstitions From All Across America* (Garden City: Doubleday and Company, 1986).

B.A. Botkin, "Don't Hit That Post Again," in *A Treasury of New England Folklore* (New York: Crown Publishers, 1947).

David Holt and Bill Mooney, "A Rude Awakening," in *Spiders in the Hairdo* (Little Rock: August House, 1999).

Henri Pourrat, "The Tale of the Dangerous Post," in *Treasury of French Folk Tales* (New York: Houghton Mifflin, 1953).

GERTRUDE FRANKLIN HORN ATHERTON

1. Elinor Richey, "Gertrude Atherton," in *Eminent Women of the West* (Berkeley: Howell-North Books, 1975), 104.

2. Emily Wortis Leider, *California's Daughter: Gertrude Atherton and Her Times* (Stanford, CA: Stanford University Press, 1991), 58.

3. Ibid., 59.

4. Gertrude Atherton, *Adventures of a Novelist* (New York: Liveright, 1932), 93.

5. Leider, *California's Daughter,* 64.

6. Ibid., 65.

7. Richey, "Gertrude Atherton," 117.

PERFECT JUSTICE

"Perfect Justice" is my version of an "urban legend," the type of story that seems to simultaneously appear across the country. Urban legends are told during coffee breaks, sent over e-mail, and sometimes even written down in books. I heard this story for years before I finally found it recorded in print and in America OnLine's Urban Legends.

SOURCES INCLUDE:

Tom Burnam, *More Misinformation* (New York: Lippincott and Crowell, 1980).

David Holt and Bill Mooney, "The $100 Corvette," in *Spiders in the Hairdo* (Little Rock: August House, 1999).

MARILYN NICHOLS KANE

1. Karen S. Schneider, "Daddy Meanest," *People Weekly,* 4 September 1995, 40–45.

2. Ibid.

3. Ibid.

4. Ibid.

5. Lynda Richardson, "Failure to Support Children Earns Man 6 Months in Jail," *New York Times,* 7 November 1996, Metro ed., B7(N).

6. Anne Wallace Allen for Associated Press, "Auction: for Child Support," *Seattle Times,* 18 August 1996.

THE OLD WOMAN AND THE MAIDS

SOURCES INCLUDE:

Aesop, "The Mistress and Her Servants," in *Aesop's Fables* (New York: Doubleday, 1919).

———"The Old Woman and Her Maids," in *The Great Fables of All Nations,* ed. Manuel Komroff (New York: Tudor Publishing Company, 1928).

GRANDMOTHER AND THE ROOSTER

1. Washington Pioneer Project, *Told by the Pioneers,* vol. 1 (Washington: Works Projects Administration, 1938), 111–112.

THE OLD WOMAN AND THE TENGU

SOURCES INCLUDE:

Fanny Hagin Mayer, "What Are You Most Scared Of?" in *Ancient Tales in Modern Japan* (Bloomington: Indiana University Press, 1984).

Garrett Bang, "Patches," in *Men from the Village Deep in the Mountains and Other Japanese Folk Tales* (New York: Macmillan, 1973).

Yoshiko Uchida, "The Terrible Black Snake's Revenge," in *The Sea of Gold and Other Tales from Japan* (New York: Charles Scribner's Sons, 1965).

LYDIA BARRINGTON DARRAGH

I found several accounts of this story, including one by Lydia Darragh's daughter Ann. The accounts differ in how and to whom the message was delivered.

1. "Lydia Darragh," in *The Philadelphia Campaign 1777* (Independence Hall Association, 1997), [http://www.ushistory.org/march/bio/lydia.htm]. This material is copyrighted by, and used with permission of, the Independence Hall Association. For further information, visit the

Independence Hall Association's Home Page on the World Wide Web at http://www.ushistory.org.

2.   Kemp P. Battle, "Lydia Darragh Will Not Tell a Lie," in *Hearts of Fire: Great Women of American Lore and Legend* (New York: Harmony Books, 1997), 135.

3.   Jack Briggs, "Lydia Darragh," in *Many Voices: True Tales from America's Past,* ed. Mary C. Weaver (Jonesborough, TN: National Storytelling Press, 1995), 21.

4.   "Lydia Darragh," www.ushistory.org.

5.   J. Clement, "Lydia Darragh," in *Noble Deeds of American Women* (Boston: Lee and Sheppard, 1875), 92.

THE DAUGHTERS OF ZELOPHEHAD

During the time of Moses, women had no property rights; therefore daughters could not inherit their fathers' property. The daughters of Zelophehad asked for their rights at a critical time, when land would be distributed upon entry into the Promised Land. See Edith Deen, "Daughters of Zelophehad," in *All the Women of the Bible* (New York: Harper and Row, 1955), 62–64.

In the first recorded lawsuit, the five daughters petitioned for their rights. They were victorious; after consulting with God, Moses wrote a new statute that applied to the twelve tribes of Israel.

The source of this passage, Numbers 26:1–11, is from *The Woman's Bible,* edited by Elizabeth Cady Stanton. Stanton (1815–1902), an organizer of the women's rights convention in Seneca Falls, believed that the Bible had been misinterpreted to justify man's domination of woman. In her introduction to *The Woman's Bible*, she explained:

> The Bible teaches that woman brought sin and death into the world, that she precipitated the fall of the race, that she was arraigned before the judgment seat of Heaven, tried, condemned and sentenced. Marriage for her was to be a condition of bondage, maternity a period of suffering and anguish, and in silence and subjection, she was to play the role of dependent on man's bounty for all her material wants, and for all the information she might desire on the vital questions of the hour, she was commanded to ask her husband at home. Here is the Bible position of woman briefly summed up.

Stanton formed a revision committee to examine the Bible; the result of their work is *The Woman's Bible*. This edition of the Bible contains only the texts pertaining to women. Comments and interpretation of the verses follow each biblical text.

The biblical text, translated by Julia Smith, a Connecticut suffragist, is doubly unique; it is the only one executed by a woman and the only one executed by one person. Julia, who was educated at Mrs. Emma Willard's seminary in Troy, New York, intended to make a literal, accurate translation from Hebrew, Greek, and Latin. She labored for seven years and then set her completed work aside for twenty years. In 1876, she paid to publish her translation. The Bibles measured seven by ten inches with large type; one style was bound in cloth and another in sheepskin. See Francis Ellen Bacon, appendix to *The Woman's Bible,* 150–151.

JULIA SMITH AND ABBY SMITH

1. Elizabeth George Speare, "Smith, Abby Hadassah and Julia Evelina," in *Notable American Woman, 1607–1950,* vol. 3, ed. Edward T. Jones (Cambridge: Harvard University Press, Belknap Press, 1971), 302–304.

2. Bruce Felton and Mark Fowler, "Abby and Julia Smith," in *Famous Americans You Never Knew Existed* (New York: Stein and Day, 1979), 146.

3. Francis Ellen Bacon, appendix to *The Woman's Bible,* ed. Elizabeth Cady Stanton (Boston: Northeastern University Press, 1993), 150–151.

HINA, THE WOMAN IN THE MOON

Hina is the mother of the god Maui. He lassoed the sun so it would slow down and dry his mother's tapa cloth. Tapa cloth is made from the inner bark of the *wauke,* the paper mulberry tree. The wauke is called a "canoe plant" because it was brought by canoes to Hawaii by the early Polynesian settlers. The trunks were stripped of bark and the outer bark peeled off. The inner bark went through a complex process of soaking and fermentation. Then women beat the fibers into cloth with heavy wooden mallets and dried it in the sun. Wauke plants were abundantly grown in Hawaii, but since the introduction of imported fabrics, this ancient plant is rarely found.

A Chinese legend about a woman named Ch'ang-o is similiar to the Hina legend. Ch'ang-o was married to Ki, the archer. Ki received a brew of immortality after he shot down ten suns that threatened to scorch the earth. Because Ki was a violent, abusive husband, Ch'ang-o drank the brew to keep him from living forever. Then she escaped his wrath by taking refuge on the moon; she became a goddess who protects children. See Susan Levitt, "The Year of the Gold Hare," in *We'moon '99* (Estacada, OR: Mother Tongue Ink, 1998), 28.

SOURCES INCLUDE:

Suzanne Barchers, "The Woman in the Moon," in *Wise Women* (Englewood, CO: Libraries Unlimited, 1990).

Padraic Colum, "Hina, the Woman in the Moon," in *Legends of Hawaii* (New Haven: Yale University Press, 1937).

Merlin Stone, "Hina of the Moon," in *Ancient Mirrors of Womanhood* (Boston: Beacon Press, 1990).

TINA TURNER

1. Tina Turner with Kurt Loder, *I, Tina* (New York: William Morrow, 1986), 16.

2. Ibid., 133.

3. Ibid., 192.

4. Cheo Tyehimba, "Tina's Independence Day," *Entertainment Weekly,* 2 August 1996, 72.

5. "Ike Turner Talks About Ex-Wife Tina and His New Fiancée," *Jet,* 27 September 1993, 58–61.

6. Edna Gundersen, "Wildest Dreams Do Come True," *USA Today,* 15 May 1997.

BIDDY EARLY'S BOTTLE

SOURCES INCLUDE:

Lady Gregory, "Seers and Healers: Biddy Early," in *Visons and Beliefs in the West of Ireland* (Gerrards Cross, Buckinghamshire: Colin Smythe, 1992).

Edmund Lenihan, "Telling and Foretelling," in *In Search of Biddy Early* (Dublin: Mercier Press, 1987).

Diarmuid MacManus, "Biddy Early," in *Irish Earth Folk* (New York: Devin-Adair Company, 1959).

Meda Ryan, *Biddy Early: The Wise Woman of Clare* (Dublin: Mercier Press, 1978).

ZSUZSANNA EMESE BUDAPEST

1. Susan Bridle, "Daughter of the Goddess: An Interview with Z. Budapest," *What is Enlightenment?* Fall/Winter 1996. I found this article online at [http://www.moksha.org/wie/j10/z.html].

2. Z. Budapest, *Summoning the Fates: A Woman's Guide to Destiny* (New York: Harmony, 1998), 207.

3. Ibid., 207.

4. Z. Budapest, *The Grandmother of Time* (San Francisco: Harper, 1989), 226.

5. In *Spiritual Psychic Science Church of Truth v. City of Azusa*, 217 Cal. Rptr. 225 (1985), a case not related to Budapest's conviction, the California Supreme Court struck down a city ordinance prohibiting fortunetelling. The City of Azusa had a municipal law that made it a crime to practice fortunetelling, card or tea reading, palmistry, astrology, etc. for payment. The Court said such an ordinance violated the California Constitutional provision that every person may freely speak, write, and publish his or her sentiments. However, the Court also found that although fortunetelling was protected communication, it could be subject to regulation.

CLEVER GRETEL

Perhaps the wine Clever Gretel sipped was a dandelion wine of her own making. Perhaps, when she went walking in her red shoes, she picked dandelion flowers. Or she might have grown them in her kitchen garden. Dandelions were cultivated in European gardens for hundreds of years. Their flowers were used in tea and wine; their leaves were used in salads or cooked as greens. The plants were brought by settlers from Europe to North America for food and medicine.

Perhaps, if Clever Gretel drank too much wine or ate too much fatty food, she made a tea or coffee from dandelion root. The root extract is a tonic that cleanses the liver and improves the metabolizing of fat.

SOURCES INCLUDE:

Walter De la Mare, "Clever Gretel," in *Tales Told Again* (New York: Alfred A. Knopf, 1955).

James R. Foster, "The Partridges," in *Great Folktales of Wit and Humor* (New York: Harper and Brothers, 1955).

Jakob Ludwig Karl Grimm and Wilheim Karl Grimm, "Clever Gretel," in *Grimms' Tales For Young and Old,* trans. Ralph Manheim (New York: Doubleday, Anchor Press, 1977).

ALICE B. TOKLAS

1. Catherine R. Stimpson, "Toklas, Alice Babette," in *Notable American Women: The Modern Period* (Cambridge: Harvard University Press, Belknap Press, 1980), 693–694.

2. Stephen Longstreet, "Alice Toklas and Friend," in *The Queen Bees: The Women Who Shaped America* (New York: Bobbs-Merrill Company, 1979), 141–149.

3. Alden Whitman, *The Obituary Book* (New York: Stein and Day, 1971), 111.

4. Alice B. Toklas, *The Alice B. Toklas Cookbook* (New York: Doubleday, Anchor Books, 1960), 273–274.

5. Ibid., 190.

6. Ibid., 194.

BR'ER RABBIT AND MAMMY-BAMMY BIG-MONEY

In Shakespeare's comedy, *A Midsummer Night's Dream,* Oberon, the king of the fairies, squeezes the juice of a flower on the eyelids of Titania, the sleeping queen of the fairies. Titania wakes, sees, and falls in love with Nick Bottom the Weaver who is wearing a donkey's head. The humble flower, made magical by Cupid's arrow, is named love-in-idleness, the Elizabethan name for pansy. The wild pansy, which is a widespread weed in Europe and the United States, is also called Johnny Jump-up, Heartsease, or Cupids's Flower.

Br'er Rabbit and Mammy-Bammy Big-Money:

The rice-bird, a member of the blackbird family, is also called the white-winged blackbird or bobolink. This gregarious songbird was hunted by the rice farmers in Louisiana and Mississippi because of its tendency to steal crops from the fields.

Br'er Rabbit was a hero of tales brought to America from Africa; he was a trickster who outsmarted those who oppressed him. Author Julius Lester says "Br'er Rabbit is a symbol of how black people responded to slavery."

Elements from the following separate tales were combined into this tale:

Joel Chandler Harris, "Brother Rabbit's Love Charm," in *The Complete Tales of Uncle Remus,* comp. Richard Chase (Boston: Houghton Mifflin Company, 1955).

Julius Lester, "Brer Rabbit's Luck," in *The Tales of Uncle Remus* (New York: Dial Books, 1987).

———"Mammy-Bammy Big-Money Takes Care of Brer Wolf," in *More Tales of Uncle Remus* (New York: Dial Books, 1988). A retelling in standard English of Joel Chandler Harris' *The Complete Tales of Uncle Remus.*

Jackie Torrence, "Mammy Bammy Big Money," in *The Importance of Pot Liquor* (Little Rock: August House, 1994).

MARIE LAVEAU

1. Rosemary Ellen Guiley, *The Encyclopedia of Ghosts and Spirits* (New York: FactsOnFile, 1992), 192.

2. Khephra Burns, "The Queen of Voodoo," *Essence*, May 1992, 80.

3. "Voodoo," in *American Folklore and Legend*, ed. Jane Polley (Pleasantville, NY: Reader's Digest Association, 1978), 57.

4. Lyle Saxon, *Famous New Orleans* (New York: D. Appleton-Century Company, 1935), 243.

5. Ibid., 244.

6. Guiley, *Ghosts and Spirits*, 193.

7. Ibid., 195.

8. Lynn Sherr and Jurate Kazickas, *Susan B. Anthony Slept Here: A Guide to American Women's Landmarks* (New York: Random House, 1994), 170.

9. I found "Make a Love Wish on Marie Laveau's Tomb," on the Internet at [http://www.spellmaker.com/marie.htm].

10. Guiley, *Ghosts and Spirits*, 195.

THE GYPSY WOMAN

Flax, a graceful plant with turquoise blue blossoms, falls under the protection of the goddess Holda, who, in Teutonic mythology, first taught mortals how to grow, spin, and weave it. Its cultivation reaches back to the remotest periods of history. Linen cloth was found in Egyptian tombs, and fibers ten thousand years old were discovered among Neolithic remains in Switzerland. Flax has been cultivated in all temperate and tropical regions for so many centuries that its geographical origin cannot be determined. It readily escapes from cultivation and is found in a semi-wild condition in all the countries where it is grown.

SOURCE: Katharine M. Briggs, "The Gipsy Woman," in *British Folktales* (New York: Pantheon Books, 1977).

Other folktales with the theme of old or reformed women convincing a husband not to let his wife spin include:

Dorothy Sharp Carter, "The Three Fairies," in *Greedy Mariani* (New York: Atheneum, 1974). Puerto Rico.

Jakob Ludwig Karl Grimm and Wilheim Karl Grimm, "The Three Spinners," in *Grimms' Tales For Young and Old*, trans. Ralph Manheim (New York: Doubleday, Anchor Press, 1977). Germany.

Bertha L. Gunterman, "The Sunbeam Sprites," in *Castles in Spain* (New York: Longmans, Green and Company, 1930). Spain.

Joseph Jacobs, "Habetrot and Scantlie Mab," in *More English Fairy Tales* (New York: G.P. Putnam's Sons, n.d.). England.

Gyula Ortuary, "Pantsy-Mantsy," in *Hungarian Folk Tales* (Budapest: Corvina, 1962). Hungary.

Ann Simley, "The Spinning Wheel," in *Stories to Tell and Read Aloud* (Minneapolis: Burgess Publishing Company, 1962). India.

William Butler Yeats, "The Lazy Beauty and her Aunts," in *Irish Folk Stories and Fairy Tales* (New York: Grosset and Dunlap, 1974). Ireland.

SARAH G. BAGLEY

1. Bess Beatty, "Textile/Apparel Workers," in *The Reader's Companion to U.S. Women's History* (New York: Houghton Mifflin Company, 1998), 590.

2. Harriet H. Robinson, *Loom and Spindle,* rev. ed. (Kailua, HI: Press Pacifica, 1976), 19.

3. Robert McHenry, ed., *Liberty's Women* (Springfield, MA: G. & C. Merriam Company, 1980), 16.

4. Christine Lunardini, *What Every American Should Know About Women's History* (Holbrook, MA: Bob Adams, 1994), 61–62.

5. Lynn Sherr and Jurate Kazickas, *Susan B. Anthony Slept Here: A Guide to American Women's Landmarks* (New York: Random House, 1994), 209.

6. Madeleine B. Stern, "Sarah G. Bagley," in *We the Women* (Lincoln: University of Nebraska, 1962), 87.

WHY CAT LIVES WITH WOMAN

SOURCES INCLUDE:

Hugh Tracey, "The Cat Who Came Indoors," in *The Lion on the Path* (London: Routledge and Kegan Paul, 1967).

Eleanor Heady, "Why Cats Live With Women," in *When the Stones Were Soft: East African Fireside Tales* (New York: Funk and Wagnalls, 1968).

MABEL STARK

Perhaps Mabel Stark gained the affection of the tigers by giving them catnip. Catnip, a wildflower native to Eurasia and Africa, is generally cultivated as an herb. Settlers who brought it to America used it to make tea to treat colds and digestive problems. A member of the mint family, catnip is covered with spires of tiny lavender flowers and blue gray foliage. The plant is called catnip because cats are intoxicated by the fragrant oils in its leaves and stems. Folklore says that by giving catnip to your cat, you will create a psychic bond between the two of you.

1. Fred Bradna with Hartzell Spence, *The Big Top: My Forty Years with the Greatest Show on Earth* (New York: Simon and Schuster, 1952), 315.

2. Mabel Stark with Gertrude Orr, *Hold That Tiger* (Caldwell, ID: Caxton Printers, 1938), 13.

3. Ibid., 18.

4. Ibid., 13.

5. Bradna, *The Big Top,* 207.

6. John Culhane, *The American Circus: An Illustrated History* (New York: Henry Holt and Company, 1990), 181.

THE BUCCA-BOO

SOURCES INCLUDE:

Ruth Manning-Sanders, "Bucca Dhu and Bucca Gwidden," in *Peter and the Piskies* (New York: Roy Publishers, 1958).

Katharine M. Briggs, "The White Bucca and the Black," in *British Folktales* (New York: Pantheon Books, 1970).

POKER ALICE

1. Lynn Sherr and Jurate Kazickas, *Susan B. Anthony Slept Here: A Guide to American Women's Landmarks* (New York: Random House, 1994), 418.

2. Hank Messick and Burt Goldblatt, *The Only Game in Town* (New York: Thomas Y. Crowell Company, 1976), 54.

3. Grace Ernestine Ray, *Wily Women of the West* (San Antonio: Naylor Company, 1972), 82–84.

AUNT MISERY

SOURCES INCLUDE:

Dorothy Sharp Carter, "Why Misery Remains in the World," in *Greedy Mariani* (New York: Atheneum, 1974).

Patricia Tracy Lowe, "Aunt Misery," in *The Little Horse of Seven Colors and Other Portuguese Folktales* (New York: World, 1970).

Olga Loya, "Tía Miseria," in *From Sea to Shining Sea,* ed. Amy L.Cohn (New York: Scholastic, 1993).

SADIE AND BESSIE DELANY

1. Roberta Henderson, "A Play's Invisible Character," *New York Times* Sunday, 2 April 1995, F19.

2. Sarah L. Delany and A. Elizabeth Delany with Amy Hill Hearth, preface to *The Delany Sisters' Book of Everyday Wisdom* (New York: Kodansha, 1996), 1x.

3. Ibid., 8.

4. Amy Hill Hearth, "How to Live to be 100," *Heart & Soul,* April/May 1995, 87–88.

5. Sarah L. Delany and A. Elizabeth with Amy Hill Hearth, *Having Our Say: The Delany Sisters' First 100 Years* (New York: Dell Press, 1993), 289.

6. Ibid., 246.

7. Ibid., 267.

8. Delany, Delany, and Hearth, *Everyday Wisdom,* 111.

9. Lynn Norment, "Aging Gracefully," *Ebony,* August 97, 70–73.